RESOLVING CONFLICT

With Others and Within Yourself

Gini Graham Scott, Ph.D.

Distributed in the U.S.A. by Publishers Group West; in Canada by Raincoast Books; in Great Britain by Airlift Book Company, Ltd.; in South Africa by Real Books, Ltd.; in Australia by Boobook; and in New Zealand by Tandem Press.

New Harbinger Publications, Inc.
Department B
5674 Shattuck Avenue
Oakland, CA 94609

ISBN 0-934986-81-9 (paperback)

99   98

20   19   18   17   16   15   14   13   12

Contents

Introduction

Joe had a problem. After living through the 1960s as a hippie and spending the 1970s on a quest for personal growth, he had finally settled down. In the 80s, he had a straight job as a mid-level manager in a large company. In fact, he bragged about having kept a single job for over three years. "I've just passed 1000 days," he told me when I met him.

But Joe was torn between wanting to hang onto this source of stability and trying to do something more creative. Political action particularly appealed to him. He was eager to organize the people in his community to do something about the serious social problems he observed all around him: problems of crime, police indifference and brutality, environmental pollution, and more.

Joe was held back by the various "what ifs" that plagued his mind: What if I try to do this and no one is interested? What if I succeed and find the project is taking too much time? What if I spend all this time trying to get things started, and it doesn't work, and all the time is wasted? What if other people see what I'm doing and think it's ridiculous? What if I start doing this, and I end up losing my job? And so on.

Delores had a different problem. She knew what she wanted to do and was ready to do it. But she didn't know how to proceed, so for now she felt stuck. She had been working as a secretary in a large oil company's headquarters for years. Yet now, in her mid 40s, she felt increasingly dissatisfied because she wasn't using her skills. She had a background in education, and she felt there was a major need in her company—and others like it—for employee training and development. But she had checked her local help-watch ads and hadn't found anything that seemed to match the type of work she wanted to do. Where could she go with her ideas? ... Delores didn't know.

Paul faced yet another kind of conflict. It was closer to home—in fact, it *was* his home. Paul lived in a power vacuum. He shared an old Victorian that had been turned into five apartments with four other tenants. The landlord lived off in Hawaii, and in his absence there was no one in charge. As a result, the common areas were gradually going to pot. One tenant paid a little bit less, because he was the manager, and his job was to collect the rents, handle arrangements when old tenants moved out, and find new tenants to move in. He had never been given direct responsibility for taking care of the common areas, but now a few of the tenants, including Paul, were becoming very upset. They wanted the place cleaned up and some repairs done. The manager said it wasn't his responsibility. Meanwhile, some of the other tenants said they didn't care that much what happened—and besides, it was someone else's job. Paul felt something needed to be done—but what—and who should do it?

In Laura's case, the conflict was more a matter of interoffice politics. She worked as an administrative assistant in the headquarters of a large sales organization, and she saw a chance to get ahead into a better position in another division of her company. However, the two managers she worked for were fighting among themselves, and she felt that one or both of them might do something to undermine her chances. When she spoke to a manager of the division that was hiring, he said they already had someone else in mind; but so far nothing was certain. Was it true, Laura wondered? Could she still have a chance? Were her current managers trying to keep her where she was? Did she risk losing her present position if she tried for the opening more actively? She felt torn between what she wanted and the inner upheavals in her office which might stand in her way.

Resolving Conflicts Through Conflict Management Techniques

What these four individuals had in common was the feeling of being trapped by everyday conflicts. They were so caught up by the fear of making the right choices, by their lack of information, by uncertainty, by poor communication, or by other blocks that they didn't know what to do. So they tended to hang onto the status quo, although they were clearly unsatisfied with it. And as long as the conflict blocked them, they couldn't move ahead to a better and more satisfying situation.

Yet such conflicts can be readily overcome. The key is to regard them as problems to be resolved: first by identifying the source of the problem, and then by applying the appropriate problem solving techniques. For example, techniques like creative visualization might be used to examine the reasons for the problem; brainstorming might be used to come up with alternatives; automatic writing might be used to ask the inner self for reactions to these possibilities; and mental imaging might be used to ask an inner expert for advice in making choices. Finally, mental control or mind power techniques might be used to gain enough internal motivation or control to put new solutions into practice. Each person has the ability to act with resolve to overcome his or her conflicts.

At times, it can take an outside advisor or consultant to assess the situation and suggest conflict remedies. An outsider has the advantage of being detached from the situation. He or she doesn't have the emotions and fears which can stand in the way of seeing or solving the conflict. The outsider can look at the dynamics of the problem dispassionately and suggest appropriate techniques to come up with solutions that will work.

Of course, anyone in a conflict can learn to use these techniques by learning to look at the conflict as an outsider might assess it. He can look within himself and at the dynamics of the situation to discover the sources of the conflict. And then he can think of alternative approaches, decide on the best strategy, and put that solution to the conflict into practice.

Let's look back at the conflicts the four people described earlier were experiencing. For all of them the solution was present in the conflict, if only they were able to separate themselves from the situation enough to see it.

Joe, for instance, was overloading the conflict situation for himself by building up all sorts of unnecessary fears. These stood in his way of doing anything. He was thinking he had to literally guarantee himself a clear picture of the success he would achieve if he embarked on his desired project at all, rather than taking the task one step at a time.

Thus, when I worked with him on coming up with solutions, I got him to look at his proposed political action campaign in stages, and to look at each phase as a learning process. This way, he didn't feel he had to accomplish a successful campaign when he first started. Since this was the first time he was doing anything like this, he could concentrate on and feel good about learning what to do. He could take what he had learned and apply it to a subsequent organizational campaign. This way, if the project didn't work out, he wouldn't feel he was wasting his time. He could think about what worked and what didn't, and create an improved plan for the future.

At the same time, I helped him work out a reasonable way of managing his concerns about the time needed to launch the project versus his time on his own job. First, he needed to budget the amount of time he was honestly willing to spend on the new project. Then, he could postpone further involvement until he felt ready to leave his job, as he eventually hoped to do. He did not have to make this decisive commitment now. He could wait and see. By the same token, as other people got involved in his organizational efforts, he coud think about delegating tasks to others; he didn't have to do it all.

I also helped Joe look more rationally at his fears about what others would think. He needed to step away from these concerns, which were based on a desire to present an image of someone who never made mistakes. If he looked at the whole process as a learning exercise, where he was allowed to be imperfect, then his fears about what others would think—really a projection of his own critic judging himself— melted away.

Once these fear barriers were gone, Joe's next step was figuring out what to do to put his organizational ideas into action. Who should he contact? What was the first step? The challenge now was to come up with ideas and alternatives, and together we brainstormed. Maybe he could put together some flyers and place them around the neighborhood. Maybe he could write a short ad and place it in a weekly city paper that featured local political reporting, local events, and an extensive classified section with lots of personal ads. He could have a small organizing meeting with people responding to these flyers and ads, and then go from there. By getting rid of the "what ifs" and fears standing in the way and by creating an action plan, Joe was readying himself to move on and actually do something. It was time to stop dreaming about what he might do, feeling stuck, and doing nothing.

Delores also needed to take constructive action before she could move ahead with her ideas to combine business and education. The major source of her problem was a lack of information about what she wanted to do. Once she realized this, she was able to prepare herself to act. For example, as we discussed her problem, it became obvious she had been looking in the wrong job categories in the help wanted columns, since she had been looking for jobs under education. She was really looking for something known in business circles as "training," and she should look there. Also, there were organizations for people in training, and she could easily go to some of these groups and find leads to potential jobs. She might even be able to create her own job and approach companies as an independent consultant offering programs in education and training. There was suddenly more than one attractive avenue to pursue.

In Paul's case, he had to accept a more active role than he expected. Since the conflict grew out of a power vacuum and the lack of communication between the five tenants, Paul had to somehow step into that vacuum. He needed to open up channels of communication, since *he* most wanted to solve the problem. Otherwise, if he and the other tenants felt the conflict was not important enough, the problem would go on. What could he do? We brainstormed some possibilities. He could approach each one of the tenants directly, sit down and talk to them, and try to work out a solution. He could send out a letter proposing a meeting of the group to decide what to do. When Paul observed that a few of the tenants felt the problem was important, while the rest of the tenants felt they had no legal responsibility to do anything—and in fact did not. Paul had to face the fact that perhaps the tenants who wanted the community areas kept clean might have to do it themselves. By looking at the conflict in a problem solving mode, Paul was well on his way to coming up with some solutions, instead of griping about the gradual deterioration of the premises, which had been going on for several months.

In Laura's case, the difficulty revolved around her lack of knowledge about the political waters of her office—and her lack of communication with the various personalities involved. She needed to become more familiar with the political climate through careful conversations with her managers and with the people in the other division where she worked. She had to let people know in a diplomatic way what she wanted. And she had to learn what real skills were needed for the job she desired so that she could demonstrate her proficiency—if in fact she had those skills. Laura had been silent and resentful for too long about the opportunity she saw slipping away. She needed to do something quickly to determine the best way to approach getting the new job, if she decided she was qualified to get it.

Applying Conflict Management Techniques to Any Problem

The conflict management techniques used with Joe, Delores, Paul, and Laura are tools that anyone can learn to use on his or her own. They will help resolve virtually any type of problem: whether inner conflict or conflict between people.

The whole process starts by looking over your major conflicts and determining which ones to start with. This involves setting priorities, since you can only work effectively on a few conflicts at a time.

Then, too, it is important to look at the reasons for the conflicts and to pinpoint the *source* of tension. This way you can come up with the appropriate solutions. For instance, some conflicts are due to circumstances in the situation; others to the personalities of the people involved; still others may point to a recurring behavior pattern or attitude which trigger recurring conflicts.

It is helpful to have a picture of some of the most common reasons for conflicts. Models can suggest particular strategies and approaches to use in attacking your own similar conflicts. In the chapters that follow, you'll see examples of conflict between people resulting from poor communication and mis-understandings; different agendas, interests, and values; political power struggles in a group situation; wrong assumptions about others' actions; a lack of empathy with others' needs and wants; and problems arising from dealing with difficult or crazy-making people, who must be handled in a certain diplomatic way. Just as those represent the most common interpersonal conflicts, you'll also discover ways of dealing with common *internal* conflicts such as being held back by fears, a lack of information, a belief that one can't do something, or mixed messages from the heart and the mind. Many of the examples will probably strike some familiar chords.

There are various techniques you will learn to use to uncover reasons and sources behind such problems. The techniques include creative visualization, mental imaging, automatic writing, and even ask-the-expert techniques. Once you uncover the first level of reasons and sources, it may become necessary to go back even further to get to the underlying block. For example, if a person expresses a fear about doing what he or she needs to do to solve a conflict, it may be necessary to look at the reasons the person has that fear. Or if it appears that another person is standing in the way of achieving a goal, it may become necessary to ask why that person is acting as a block or whether that person needs to be there at all.

Once the underlying reasons and sources for the conflict are uncovered, the next step is to correct the problem with the appropriate response. For example, if the conflict is caused by poor communication or a complete lack of communication, the obvious response is to find ways to open up communication. If the conflict is due to different agendas, the response becomes one of negotiating compromises and looking for solutions where both people benefit: win-win solutions. If there are difficult people involved, such as hostile-aggressives, complainers, or negative people who put down everything, the response involves meeting their actions with the appropriate defensive strategies. And if your own fears or indecisions are standing in the way, the solution lies in coming up with methods to overcome these blocks so you can move on.

Dreaming up options and alternatives can be a liberating experience, as well as a source of productive solutions. In fact, if you look on most conflicts as problems that can be turned into possibilities, you'll have found all sorts of new routes to personal, interpersonal, and organizational growth. A conflict can tell you what you need to learn about yourself; it can provide insights into what is wrong in a relationship so it might change to become more fulfilling; and it can indicate what kind of organizational barriers to productivity exist so these can be overcome.

1

The Rational-Intuitive Method for Resolving Conflicts

The possibility for conflict exists everywhere. Conflicts arise out of everyday differences of opinion, disagreements, and the interplay of different ideas, needs, drives, wishes, lifestyles, values, beliefs, interests, and personalities of people. Yet conflicts are more than just debates or negotiations. They represent an escalation of everyday competition and discussion into an arena of hostile or emotion-provoking encounters that strain personal or interpersonal tranquility, or both.

For example, you get a bill from the landlord which is higher than you think it should be. You go to the landlord to discuss it. He argues that the increase is justified because his own taxes have been increased and there has been a rise in the cost of gas and electricity. Is this a conflict? Probably it's more accurately described at this point as a disagreement or a difference of opinion. But then, as with any difference of opinion or divergence in personal needs and goals, there is always the potential that a real conflict might develop if the emotions become engaged or hostility is expressed. Say you claim you won't pay the increase; the landlord threatens eviction; you raise complaints about the landlord's past failures to fix problems with the plumbing; and so on. The result is that at some point, as opposing positions are expressed more strongly and emotions heat up, this discussion turns into a conflict. It becomes a heated verbal combat based on competing or opposing interests, and in some cases.

This kind of scenario plays itself out again and again at all levels in human relationships—between spouses, lovers, friends, parents and children, business associates, relatives, neighbors, everybody. And it can occur internally as well when you face opposing desires and needs that pull you in different directions.

When you don't know how to deal with these situations, the uncomfortable feelings generated by the conflict can be destructive to you and the relationship. The actual outcome of the conflict can be even more unproductive and detrimental. For instance, to return to the landlord example, you might end up not only paying the increased rent, but feeling resentful toward your landlord. This might trigger further hostile encounters, leading eventually to your moving out or to your landlord evicting you. In the worst case, the initial discussion might actually escalate from an exchange of heated words to physical violence. On the other hand, with proper strategy, the potential conflict could be steered into an alternate more favorable resolution. The landlord might agree to defer any increase while you agree to seek ways to cut down the landlord's gas and electricity costs for the apartment. You might help out by taking on some informal management responsibilities, which is what the landlord really needs right now.

In other words, with the proper conflict management skills, potential conflicts can be averted or defused—and even turned into a positive source for improved interpersonal relationships and personal growth. The key is not to *avoid* conflict, which is potentially inherent in all social interactions and in all personal choices we make, but to recognize it and manage it skillfully to produce the best outcome.

An ideal technique for doing this is the rational-intuitive method of conflict resolution. In essence, this method involves using your reason and your intuition to make choices about how to react in conflict situations. You base your approach on the circumstances, the personalities, interests, and needs of the people involved, and on your own goals, interests, and needs. This is a powerful approach, because at its heart, any serious conflict engages the emotions of its participants. Therefore, one of the first steps in resolving conflict is to defuse the negative emotions generated by the conflict—both your own and the other people's. Reason and intuition, rather than emotions, are needed to counter these feelings. Otherwise, if you react from your own feelings to these already heightened feelings, you will only contribute to further raising the emotional tension level instead of defusing it.

Once emotions are defused, you can use your reason or intuition, as appropriate, to figure out possible resolutions acceptable to all involved. Suppose the problem seems resolvable now. You might begin by figuring out *strategies* for arriving at possible resolutions. But if this is an extremely difficult situation, and there is no realistic way of resolving it or defusing emotions at the time, you might use this rational-intuitive method to decide that the best thing to do right now is walk away. For properly employed, avoidance can be as effective a choice as working out the problem.

Once you've learned to understand, assess, and make these choices in the conflict or potential conflict situations you encounter, you will optimize your ability to gain what you want from the particular conflict. Also, you might have something to gain from the people with whom you are in conflict. And if a particular conflict is a barrier to something you want, by overcoming it you might achieve your goal, too.

This chapter describes the basic rational-intuitive model, and then subsequent chapters describe how to use it in handling different stages and types of conflicts. The many examples will help you see how the method might be applied in various conflict situations.

The Rational-Intuitive Conflict Management Model

The basic way to use the rational-intuitive approach to managing conflict is to look on any conflict situation as a problem or potential problem to be solved. Then, you select the appropriate problem solving techniques from an arsenal of possible strategies for dealing with the conflict. The strategy you select will depend on what stage the conflict is at (potential conflict, developing conflict, open conflict), the importance of a particular resolution of the conflict to you, an assessment of what the other person needs and wants, and the types of emotions released by the conflict. Then, having selected the appropriate technique, you determine the best way to apply it. The choices you make depend on both your ability to assess the situation and the alternatives rationally, your ability to intuit what option is best for the situation, and your ability to put that choice into action.

Whenever you find yourself in a conflict or potential conflict situation, you should go through a quick checklist (like the one that follows). Depending on your answer, choose the appropriate response. It may take some time to learn to do this, because at first you will have to think your reactions through. But in time, as you use this approach, you will find that the choices come spontaneously. It's like flashing through all the options in your mind in a moment, and then intuitively choosing the ones you want to employ in a particular case.

The following chart describes the questions to ask and strategies to use. Subsequent chapters describe how and when to use each of these strategies in more detail, so when you are in a conflict situation yourself you can review your options and decide the best ones to choose.

Questions To Ask	**Strategies To Use**
1) Are emotions causing the conflict or standing in the way of a resolution? If yes:	
a) What are these emotions?	a) Techniques to calm the feelings on both sides, so you can work out solutions/agreements.
(1) Anger? If so, whose?	
(a) The other person's?	a) Techniques to cool down or deflect the anger, such as empathic listening, letting the other person vent his or her anger, and statements to sooth hurt feelings or correct misunderstandings generating anger.
(b) Your own?	b) Techniques to channel or control your anger, such as short-

Questions To Ask	Strategies To Use
	term venting, deflection, and visualization to release anger.
(2) Mistrust? If so, whose?	
(a) The other person's?	a) Techniques to overcome mistrust.
(b) Your own?	b) Techniques to assess the accuracy of this mistrust or deal with it openly and productively.
(3) Fear? If so, whose?	
(a) The other person's?	a) Techniques to reduce fear.
(b) Your own?	b) Techniques to assess the accuracy of this fear or deal with it openly and productively.
(4) Other emotions? (i.e., jealousy, guilt, etc.)	
(a) The other person's?	a) Techniques to calm the other person.
(b) Your own?	b) Techniques to calm yourself.
2) What are the underlying reasons for the conflict?	a) Looking for real needs and wants.
a) What does the other person really need and want?	a) Direct communication to ask the person to outline reasons, needs, and wants if possible.
	b) Intuitive and sensing techniques to pick up the underlying reasons if the person isn't willing to speak or if the person isn't self-aware enough to recognize these underlying needs and wants.
b) What do you really need and want?	a) Self-examination to determine your real desires and needs if you aren't already clear about them.
	b) Intuitive and sensing techniques to consider underlying goals.

Questions To Ask	**Strategies To Use**
3) Is the conflict due to a misunderstanding? Whose?	a) Techniques for overcoming the misunderstanding through better communication.
a) The other person's?	a) Techniques to explain and clarify.
b) Your own?	b) Techniques to be open and receptive to the other person's explanations.
c) Both or uncertain?	c) A combination of techniques to explain and clarify and to be open and receptive to the other's explanations.
4) Is the conflict due to someone failing to take responsibility for some action? A past action? A future action? An agreement to do something?	a) Techniques to determine who is responsible and to gain acceptance for this responsibility.
a) The other person's responsibility?	a) Techniques to get the other person to acknowledge responsibility and agree to do something.
b) Your own responsibility?	b) Techniques to recognize and acknowledge this.
5) What kind of conflict styles would be most suitable to use in this situation?	a) Assessing the available conflict styles and choosing between them, based on: 1) the conflict styles you prefer; 2) the conflict styles you feel the others feel most comfortable with; 3) the conflict styles that would be most effective under the circumstances.
a) Is it possible to reach a win-win solution?	a) Using negotiation and discussion to achieve a resolution through compromise or collaboration.
b) Is the conflict worth resolving now at all?	b) Choosing avoidance to avoid the issue now.

Questions To Ask	Strategies To Use
c) Are there power considerations that can effect the resolution of the conflict? Who is more powerful?	
(1) The other person.	a) Using accommodation or offers to compromise.
(2) You.	b) Using competition or offers to compromise.
6) Are there special personality factors to be considered in resolving the conflict?	
a) Is the other person a difficult person to deal with?	a) Using techniques for dealing with particularly difficult people.
b) Do you have special personality needs you need met (i.e.: needs for recognition)?	b) Techniques to express your needs effectively.
7) What kind of alternatives and solutions are possible?	a) Coming up with ideas yourself or getting other parties to make suggestions.
a) What alternatives and solutions are available?	a) Brainstorming and creative visualization to come up with ideas.
b) How can this problem be turned into an opportunity?	b) Brainstorming and creative visualization.
c) What are the best outcomes?	c) Prioritizing the possibilities.

Part I

Clearing Out the Emotional Closet

2

Overcoming Two of the Major Sources of Conflict: Anger and Mistrust

This chapter describes some cases involving anger and mistrust, and illustrates how each situation might be resolved. Then it suggests how you might overcome such barriers yourself.

Putting Anger Aside

Anger can build up over time in any relationship. There can be real hurts, imagined hurts, and new hurts on top of past hurts, which keep mounting up. Attempts to express the anger can sometimes lead to even more hurts. Your anger might feed the other person's anger, and his yours, until you scream, or stop talking entirely (or start talking behind each other's backs!). There can seem to be no way to stop the escalating spiral. Each person thinks the other is acting out of bad will, and sees each new action, no matter how innocent, as another attack.

An example of this happened to Mona, Dennis, and some of Mona's neighbors. Mona had been living in a building with very low rent and very thin walls for about 15 years. One problem was that her lifestyle created a fair amount of noise, since she was an energetic, heavy woman, who worked odd hours as a computer programmer. At times she banged the cupboards and the doors, walked around on uncarpeted floors in wooden shoes, and once decided to beat out her carpet at midnight. The paper-thin walls in the building didn't help. When some of the tenants tried to approach Mona about her noise, Mona became angry—in fact, downright hysterical according some tenants. She yelled back at the other tenants, accusing them of making noise themselves and blaming her unfairly. And then she would storm back into her apartment and slam the door.

In turn, Mona had her own complaints. For instance, her next door neighbor Dennis once had a very sick friend stay with him for about two weeks. While the man was dying, Mona could hear the noisy oxygen machine whirring and the man moaning at all hours of the night. Although she was sympathetic, she couldn't sleep. She made Dennis angry in return by banging on his walls late at night, when the noise became unbearable. When Dennis asked her to be patient, because the man was suffering so much and had only a few days of life left, she responded bluntly: "Well, I'll die myself if I don't get any sleep soon."

Her relationships with the other tenants and her landlord were deteriorating, too. One elderly woman, Mildred, thought Mona made just about every loud noise she heard in the building, and reported her to the landlord. But when Mona brought her own complaints to the landlord about other tenants—about Dennis, and about the people below her whose unpleasant cooking smells rose up into her apartment through the vent— she felt they were ignored. The landlord seemed to think that Mona was responsible for everything that went wrong in the place.

I met Mona when I was participating on a neighborhood conflict resolution panel for Community Boards in San Francisco. The situation had become desperate. Mona's landlord had given her an eviction notice, which she was fighting. She wanted to stay, since in spite of it all she liked her apartment and the low rent. She felt she had some valid gripes of her own about the other tenants; but no one listened to her. Everyone seemed to think she was nuts. The good part was that everyone, including Mona, was willing to talk about the situation to try to resolve it.

At first, it looked like they weren't going to make it. Mona and Dennis started airing their long lists of complaints. Mona had actually been keeping a record of presumed offenses by other tenants, particularly Dennis, for several years, and she began to reel them off, her body rigid with anger.

They say it's me, but Dennis has been making noise that's driving me crazy. He has the radio on late at night.... He's got all his stereo equipment in his bedroom which is right next to mine.... His answering machine gets calls at odd hours, and he keeps his phone right against the wall ... He slams the door to the bathroom shower.... He's noisy at his closet. Once I heard him open it five times at 12:30 a.m.... I think I'm dealing with a pathological noise maker....

And I've been trying not to make noise ... but everyone blames me .... I go to work worn out from this situation.... There's no way to get away from the noise....

For about 15 minutes she want on, angrily airing gripes that had been festering over the years. Then, Dennis came right back with his own gripes about her.

Ridiculous. She claims I'm making all this noise. Hah. I hardly get any calls when she says ... I'm not even home that much, and almost no one calls. They all know my schedule at work. ...

And when I once asked her for her patience about my sick friend, she yelled at me.... She's called the police ... I try to talk to her, but she rants and raves. It's just an impossible situation. I wish she would move.

When Mildred and the landlord weighed in with their own complaints, things got even more tense. Hilda complained of banging doors at midnight and being called names. She spoke of other tenants who had moved. The landlord spoke of Mona's constant complaining and his own desires for quiet and peace. "That's why I finally gave up and gave her the eviction notice," he said. "I've told her not to slam the door, but she does. And she walks loudly. I've had so many complaints, I got fed up."

The tension in the room was electric. Mona bounded up. She had still more complaints she wanted to read about Dennis. She wanted to respond to the charges against her. She had so much more to say—so much anger over what had been going on for years. She was like a stick of dynamite ready to blow, and she aired her list of gripes with even more intensity, accusing the owner, Dennis, and the other tenants of even more offenses.

And then, finally, the crisis mounted to its boiling point, as Dennis got up with a frustrated outcry.

"I'm not going to listen to all this stuff anymore," he announced. "What's the point?" And with that, he bounded up and headed out the door.

Mona seemed oblivious and was ready to continue on with more of her charges. But this incident was the turning point.

"What do you really want to get out of this meeting?" one of the members of the conflict resolution group asked her. "Do you just want to dump your gripes on everyone and that's it?"

"Then we asked her if she wouldn't rather work on trying to find some solutions. "If so," we told her, "it looks like you're going to have to put your gripes aside and let go of your anger. You'll have to put all that in the past. Now is the time to think about what you can do to resolve the situation and work together peacefully. If you keep dumping all this anger, everyone is just going to get mad, and nothing is going to change. Dennis has already walked out because he doesn't want to listen. Are you willing to put your anger about the past aside and look to the future?"

At first, Mona resisted. "But," she burbled, waving her list, "they did ... she did ... he did ..."

Each time she tried to rehash old angers, we called her back.

"Are you willing to think about what you can do together in the future to resolve this problem? Are you willing to let go of your anger?"

And then, amazingly, she calmed down. She closed her book and quietly nodded yes. At once, it was like the charged electricity in the room dissipated. Mildred and the landlord, who were poised on the edges of their seats ready to take off like Dennis, moved back in their chairs. They were now willing to listen.

"What do you think you can do to help solve the problem?" one of the panelists asked Mona. "How do you think you can help to make the building more quiet?"

For the first time, Mona had some positive suggestions.

"I'll be careful about closing the door. I can wear some slippers during the day instead of my wooden shoes."

When Mildred and the landlord tried to bring up their own past angers, we stopped them too.

"She said that before, but didn't do it," said Mildred.

"She's always so noisy," said the landlord. "She's always complaining. How do we know things will be any different?"

"No, that's about the past again. Think of the future," we reminded them.

Eventually the landlord agreed to try. He would hold off on pursuing the eviction to see if the situation resolved itself, and he would speak to Dennis, too, to let him know that Mona had agreed to try. Mona would try to work towards a future solution with Dennis as well. Everyone left on a note of hope.

All still had complaints and resentments and angers from the past. But they had agreed to put them on hold, so they could go on to a more peaceful and quiet way of living together in the future.

The conflict resolution process worked for two key reasons. First, some of that anger had to be let out. The panelists had all been holding in a reservoir of anger for months, and it had swelled to the point where the dam was about to burst. But after the most violent flood waters were released, it was necessary to put the dam back up. If all the anger was let go, it would have flooded and destroyed everything.

It's like that with anger. A conflict situation can produce a great deal of anger, and there's often a need to release some before people can talk. But after a point, as in the case of Mona and her fellow tenants and landlord, the release of anger can destroy the possibility of future communication. It can make everyone even more angry, until no one wants to talk—like Dennis, who fled from the room.

You may never be in a situation where you have a conflict resolution panel to tell you to put your anger aside. But you can call a halt to it yourself.

Say you find yourself getting angrier and angrier as you air your gripes, and you find that as you do your complaints are only making the other party madder and madder. You can tell yourself: "I've got to stop. I have to let go of my anger. I have to think about what I can do to resolve this situation in the *future*. It's time to stop rehashing to past now." Or suppose someone is confronting you with some of their own complaints that make you angry. Again, tell yourself to calm down and let go.

The key in situations where the anger level is rising too much, or has been up for too long, is to let the other person know you want to stop the release of anger so you can get on to a resolution. Explain that you don't want to deny the anger or its validity, but that you want to put it on hold. In its place, you want to look at the conflict itself. What does it mean, here and now, and what can you both do differently in the future to work things out? You might say something like: "Yes, I know we are both angry, but this anger isn't getting us anywhere. I'd like to propose that we put it aside. Let's agree that some bad things happened in the past and that we feel upset with each other as a result. But now let's try to work together on what we can do in the future."

This can be a particularly useful approach if you are in conflict with someone you have to continue to deal with, such as a neighbor, a co-worker, or a spouse. You may have strong feelings of anger that built up over time. You may need to vent some of it to show that you are mad; that you feel the person has treated you badly; that you don't plan to take such behavior anymore. But when your anger begins feeding on itself and making the other person even madder, turn it off. Take control of that anger. Put it back in the bottle—like locking up a genie—so you can go on to finding a solution. Otherwise, you will remain stuck in the past with all its hurts. The situation will only get worse if you continue to dump endless anger and hostility on each other.

Thus, when you see that anger is standing in the way of reaching a solution, it's time to stop the process. Put that anger away. It may still exist; you may not be able to deny it; but you must take charge and control it. For only then, with your past anger under control, can you work together productively in the present for a solution to the conflict

Learning To Listen

Sometimes when a person feels angry or fearful, he has to get those feelings out, or they can serve as a block to a relationship.

Only after this person is heard out and reassured can ordinary non-conflict communication go on. If the person is not allowed to vent, hostility and suspicion can build, and communication can erupt into chaos and uproar.

It can be hard to listen when you're confronted by someone like this. You may want to walk away, evade the issue, or change the subject. That might even work if there is no further need to deal with that angry, fearful person. Speakers in a crowd sometimes do this. They cut off or turn away from a hostile heckler and go on to someone else. But if you want to preserve your relationship, you might have to listen while the other person vents, and calm fears that might lead to conflict. After everyone relaxes, ordinary conversation can proceed.

This happened when Gerard came to town to meet a group of students. They had studied his methods of psychic and spiritual developments with one of his trainers, Nancy. Nancy had been teaching the students for the past two months, and this was a chance to meet with the man who had originated these ideas.

One of the women who came to this small meeting at Nancy's house had some concerns about the value and legitimacy of these methods. Anna had hinted at her doubts the previous night at the final class meeting when she expressed her worries about the potential dangers of these spiritual teachings. Nancy had calmed her fears by pointing out that Gerard's teachings were designed to only help people develop and improve themselves. Also, Nancy noted that as long as she had been teaching the class herself, she had never talked about using these powers to do anything negative.

Anna had quieted down and held her questions at the time, but her worries and fears were still there. When she met Gerard, who developed these teachings, her concerns spilled over. This time there was no one in charge and no other planned program to hold her back. After the initial introductions and pleasantries were over, her barrage of questions and accusations began.

Don't you think psychic teachings can be used for evil?... How do you use them?... If you teach enlightenment, why should it be necessary to teach about psychological defense methods, too?... I've read about all of these gurus who have gotten involved in power and money trips. What are your own motivations?... Do you really have the powers you claim yourself? Are you willing to try an ESP test for me?... How can you claim your methods are only used for the good, when historically, such techniques have been used for killing and sacrifice.... Why do you want to teach others your methods? What do you get out of it? What's in it for you?

The questions went on and on for about an hour. Everyone could feel the current of hostility and fear in the air. Gerard tried to answer her as best he could. Several times he explained that his own teachings were designed to be positive. They were not in any way associated with the evil uses of power she mentioned. He was not trying to amass personal power or money through his teachings. He certainly didn't condone the anti-social use of the personal powers he taught others to develop.

But Anna still wasn't sure. How could she know his teachings really were for the good? How did she know he really had good intentions? How could she be sure he really had the powers he claimed?

Her questions continued. A few times Nancy jumped in and tried to change the subject or reassure Anna. "I think Gerard had planned to show us some special techniques tonight," she commented at one point. Later she observed, "But you've been involved in these teachings for two months, and you never saw these teachings used for any negative purpose did you?"

But Anna wasn't mollified, and she continued to grill Gerard like a cross-examiner for about an hour, until finally she felt reassured.

As she explained to Nancy after Gerard excused himself for a few minutes to take a break: "I'm sorry if I had a hidden agenda here tonight. But I had to get these questions answered. I had to feel comfortable with what Gerard is teaching before I could listen to anything else he might teach."

Then, when Gerard returned, Anna was ready to listen, and now her tone was neutral, showing she was mainly curious and no longer primarily skeptical and suspicious. She was ready to try to understand his teachings, rather than challenge Gerard's right to teach them. And so now Gerard finally began to share the ideas and techniques he had come to teach.

Later, after Anna and her husband left, Nancy asked Gerard why he had taken so much time answering Anna's questions. Why didn't he just turn them aside and get on with the ideas he had planned to present that night? How could he go to such great lengths to be patient when Anna's questions were so obviously loaded and many of her ideas and assumptions so wrong?

"Because," Gerard explained, "she had to get those feelings out. She may have been wrong, but she needed someone to listen. Otherwise, she wouldn't have been ready to listen to anyone else. Her concerns had to be dealt with before we could go on. There was no other way."

In this situation, Gerard's approach worked. When he responded to her, it sounded like he was going over the same ground again and again. But Anna needed that reassurance. Her fears were so intense that she needed to have them assuaged. Each time she brought them up again, she did so with a little less intensity, until finally they faded away. Only then could she put her attention to really listening. A slow build-up of trust and an easing of tension made her open and receptive.

Likewise, when a person acts angry and fearful about something— even if those angers and fears seem irrational—your best bet is usually simply to listen. Answer back to show you hear, and that there is no reason the person should be angry or fearful. You may feel impatient. You may hear the same concerns repeated over and over. You may want to end the conversation. But if you want to preserve the relationship, or need to achieve some resolution now, you must be patient and gentle. It takes some work, but you must learn to reassure an angry or fearful person and calm him or her down. Don't respond with your own anger: the noise and irritation level will rise, and communication will become increasingly overwhelmed by this tension. In due time, the other person's venting of anger and fear will wind down if handled correctly and then the conversation and relationship can move on.

Since your natural tendency may be to respond back in kind with your own anger, it can be very helpful to talk yourself through the beginning stages of such situations to control yourself. Think to yourself: "I must be patient. I must listen." You will learn specific distancing techniques later in this book to help yourself calm down and be receptive. As you'll find, such techniques do wonders in defusing a potentially explosive situation. Then once the fear or anger barrier is removed, you can communicate calmly and clearly to work out the original problem. Or you can go on, as Gerard did, to talk about other things.

Letting Go and Walking Away

In some situations, putting aside all built-up anger is the only way to see through to a solution. In others, letting someone vent his or her feelings can provide clear channels for communication and resolution. But in still other cases, the build-up of anger and hostility may have become so great that it may be best to let go of the relationship and walk away.

One tip-off that letting go is the answer is when merely *thinking* about a situation makes you feel all the old angers and frustrations again. Another signal is self-blame; you keep thinking, I did this or that wrong, and replay a situation over and over in your mind, thinking about what you might have done differently. Letting go may be a good idea in these situations because the conflict relationship becomes an obsession that keeps building on itself. Each time you think of it, you get madder and madder or blame yourself more and more. Letting go may also be best for conflicts in which each encounter only seems to make things worse or provokes even further feelings of anger or self- blame. Only walking away can end the cycle.

To be sure, letting go can be hard. You have an investment in each relationship, even one webbed with anger and self-blame. You may have hopes of resolving the situation and working out a fair solution the next time. But after a time, the emotional frustrations and angers caused by the relationship aren't worth it. It may be time to move on, before feelings of anger and frustration become even more destructive.

This happened to Tony. He had done a series of writing projects for a new client, Alex, referred to him by mutual friends. Tony had worked for Alex for about six months, mostly on small jobs, like short reports and presentations. Initially, everything was fine, and Alex was pleased with the work. But one day Alex gave bad instructions, so though Tony did good work, it was on the wrong job.

Alex needed to have the project done again, and Tony agreed. But who should pay? Alex tried to convince Tony to do it without charge: "You did it incorrectly." But Tony argued back, "I did it according to the incorrect instructions you gave me. You should be responsible for that."

Alex finally agreed to pay, and gave Tony new instructions. But Tony could tell that Alex still had reservations by the hesitancy with which he agreed to the arrangement and half-grunted out his "Okay." Yet, Tony went ahead with rewriting the project. He agreed to rush it through to make Alex's deadline for the project. He even got Alex's subsequent approval by phone to add a few pages to make the project even better. The initial conflict over money seemed resolved.

But then, when Alex came to pick up the project, something strange happened. Alex followed Tony into his office to get the report, asked Tony to type an extra cover page, and complimented Tony for getting the work done in time. Then, after rummaging through his pockets, Alex exclaimed: "I don't seem to have my wallet. Would a check be okay? I'll just go to the car to get it."

Alex picked up the paper, went downstairs, and returned in a few minutes to say he was dreadfully sorry, but "I don't have my checkbook either." Then, he added: "But I promise. I'll bring you the money, tonight."

Tony looked at him. Should he trust Alex? Or was Alex trying to avoid paying, despite the new agreement?

Yet Tony hesitated about expressing his reservations. Airing his suspicion would be an awful accusation. And Alex had been an occasional client for about a year, and they knew people in common. Would someone he had known and worked with for a year do something like this?

The thoughts tumbled quickly through his mind, and Tony knew he had only moments to decide what to do. He had to rush out to an appointment himself, and he knew that Alex had to have this project right away to make his own deadline. Besides, Alex already had the report in his car.

So Tony agreed. "Okay, I'll trust you," he said, though he still had his doubts. And when Alex told him: "Thank you, and I'll bring the money over tonight," he doubted that too.

Perhaps had there been more time, Tony would have expressed his suspicions. He might have mentioned that he found it hard to believe Alex had driven from his home and crossed a toll bridge without any money. He could have suggested Alex recheck his car, so there would be no losing face. Or maybe Tony could have zeroed in on what he believed were Alex's concerns about the payment of more money for something that had already been done, and have had a discussion about that. But in the rush of the moment, Tony felt he had no time. So he avoided confronting the real issue immediately, which probably would have been the proper thing to do. With everything out in the open, Tony could have expressed his concerns about trust and agreement, and Alex could have raised his concerns about money. Perhaps the two could have resolved their differences right there.

But instead Tony set a series of events in motion that led to him feeling growing anger against Alex. He felt he had been ripped off. He also felt increasing anger towards himself, because he blamed himself for trusting Alex, and not confronting the issue.

As Tony feared, Alex didn't show up that evening. When Tony finally reached him on the phone the next morning to find out why not, Alex was appropriately apologetic. Something unexpected had come up. He could come that weekend: would Tony be around? Yes, Tony agreed, he would. But again, Alex didn't show. He said he was called out of town and couldn't stop by, though he promised to call in the next few days.

When I met Tony, about a month had passed and he still hadn't gotten the money. Alex had explained that he would be out of town again for a while. What's more, Alex said he now had some problems with the new report Tony had written. So didn't Tony think it only fair not to charge him for it? "After all," Alex said: "It's not the money. I just want to be fair."

At first, Tony agreed with him. Yes, he wanted to be fair too; he wanted to give Alex the benefit of the doubt. And he even offered to do some extra work for Alex after he paid the original amount on which they agreed. In turn, Alex thanked him so much for trusting him in the first place, "when I forgot my wallet," he said.

However, once he thought about their conversation, Tony felt like he had been sucked into Alex's manipulative scheme once again. As he explained at a workshop:

> I could hardly believe it. I wanted to trust Alex. I wanted to think it would all work out. He would pay me, and then the problem would be over. But the more I thought about our conversation, the more I realized some things Alex said didn't make sense. I realized that what was wrong with his second project was that he had given me the wrong kind of materials to use and more wrong instructions; but once again, he was laying the blame for what happened on me. And I realized that even as he was thanking me for trusting him, he was finding a reason to delay paying me. When he talked about the issue not being money, I was sucked right in. But it is the money. For him it was always the money. I have no clear proof, just my suspicions, but I'm certain from everything that happened that that's what this is all about. He doesn't want to pay for something that has been his mistake from the first. But instead of admitting it, because I never confronted him on it, he used trickery and manipulation to first avoid paying me and then to get me to agree to what he did.

This interpretation didn't help Tony feel any better about what happened. In fact, he felt worse. Each time he recalled the incident, he thought about the time he had spent on the project, the money he didn't receive, the lie he had gone along with about the lost wallet, the repeated failures of Alex to show up with the money as expected, and the way Alex had tricked him again and again. He thought about what he might have done differently at each encounter along the way. He kept replaying different variations about what he should do in the future. Should he confront Alex with his original suspicions? Should he insist on getting paid and point out Alex's second mistake? Should he perhaps talk to their common friends, and find some way to put some pressure on Alex through them? Should he work with Alex in the future as if nothing had happened? Or should he just refuse to deal with Alex again until he was paid?

The actual amount involved was relatively little. Yet the circumstances surrounding the incident had caused it to take on a life of its own in Tony's mind. Besides feeling the actual financial loss, he felt victimized. Even worse, he felt it was his own fault. And whenever he thought about what he might do to resolve the situation in the future, he felt the possibility for more conflict—with Alex, with his friends, or within himself.

In a situation like this, the best resolution—and the one Tony finally chose—was to let go and put the situation behind him.

The conflict had become too convoluted and difficult to deal with, and it wasn't worth the personal turmoil it created to go on. Each subsequent contact or thought about it only triggered more anger. There seemed to be no realistic way of getting to the bottom of the situation or letting the anger out, since the whole incident was built up on a base of distrust. It was worth letting the money go to be free of the headache. The incident had grown in Tony's mind to an obsession that was only fueled further by each additional encounter and not allowed to go away. So Tony needed to let go and release; then he could learn from the situation and move on.

Is letting go the answer for you? It's worth thinking about if you have feelings of anger and hostility or self-blame that continue to grow, and if everything you do to resolve a conflict only seems to add more fuel to the flame. There are some helpful questions you can ask yourself. Is this a relationship that you need to continue? Is there much pay off in a continued relationship? If not, it might be worth it to let go. If the past conflict doesn't involve much loss, that's another signal that it might be better to cut any past losses and leave them behind. Why prolong the potential of conflict for minimal gains?

In other words, when considering whether to try to resolve a conflict or perhaps walk away, you can do a kind of cost-benefit analysis. What is the benefit of resolving the conflict compared to the benefit of walking away from it? What is the loss if you let it go compared to what you might lose if you keep trying to work for a resolution? If the costs of resolution outweigh the gains of walking away, it's better to walk away. There's no point trying to solve a conflict or maintain a relationship or regain a past loss if it's more costly to do so than to let it go. You are completely justified in simply walking away from some of the conflicts in your life.

Confronting Issues of Trust

It's important to bring any concerns about trust to the surface in the beginning. If you aren't sure whether you trust someone, it's very difficult—if not impossible—to build a good relationship. The relationship is likely to break apart over time, since a fundamental element in human interaction is missing. But if you wait to see if the relationship survives, you can't help investing part of yourself in it. This sets the stage for even more personal loss if it turns out you have good reason for not trusting this person. You have the loss resulting from the person's untrustworthiness as well as the loss from your own time and energy invested in a failed relationship. As a result, it's usually better to get out your reservations in the first place or not have the relationship at all.

This is what happened to Tony in the situation previously described. Tony wasn't sure whether to trust Alex or not, but he was afraid to confront Alex directly with his suspicions. After all, Alex was a long-term client and might be insulted. But the result of *not* airing his doubts was a growing anger and hostility against Alex. Tony continued to question and eventually obsess about Alex's motives, because he was in a state of not knowing. He ultimately had to walk away from the relationship, because it had become too painful.

Much of this pain could have been avoided if Tom had confronted Alex up front, at the first pang of doubt. In that way, the two could have discussed the underlying source of the conflict—and not the layers upon layers of behavior that subsequently covered this up. Or alternatively, if Tony didn't want to bring up the trust issue directly, he might have acted in a way that was consistent with his feelings of distrust. It was a mistake to tell Alex "I trust you," when in fact he didn't. This inconsistency only led to continued confusions down the road. If he didn't trust Alex, he should have held on to the report until Alex paid.

There are some times when it's fine to relate socially to someone you don't trust. At a cocktail party, it's only polite to talk to the person next to you. You can be sociable, and then move on. There may be no point in confronting the question of trust. Your relationship is not deep or lasting enough to warrant it.

At other times, you may need to compartmentalize your relationship with someone you don't trust. This means putting aside your feelings of distrust in a certain area to continue to have a good relationship in another area, or overall. Husbands and wives sometimes do this in the interest of family peace. Maybe they try not to fight in front of the children. Or maybe, more drastically, they say nothing if they believe their spouse is cheating on them with someone else. Continuing the relationship as it is seems a much better alternative than forcing a confrontation. Such people try to conceal their distrust and put it away.It's usually difficult and sometimes not possible to do so, but this is an example where it may seem best.

In many cases, however, it is better to acknowledge your lack of trust. Feelings of mistrust can only derail a continuing relationship. One option is to confront the situation directly and get it resolved, so you can proceed on a basis of understanding. This is usually the best plan. But if the risk of raising the issue seems too great, avoid it. But then you must act consistently with your feelings. If you don't trust someone, don't entrust them with anything. Don't make yourself vulnerable. You can be diplomatic, but act to protect yourself. You might establish some distance or delay, and take a wait and see approach. Or you might get the person to do something so you feel secure (such as leaving something of value with you while he goes to get funds). Let the other person save face. Give a reasonable explanation for your cautionary action: you might say it's your regular policy.

Ideally, of course, you want to trust. Only then will the relationship be up front and direct. But should the issue of mistrust arise, you can still get through the barrier in a number of ways if the relationship is worth continuing—you can confront it directly; compartmentalize it if you can, so any distrust is removed from a central place in the relationship; or act to protect yourself, while you deal with the person you aren't sure you trust. Still, whatever approach you choose, just realize that mistrust still serves to some extent as a barrier. So try to eliminate or reduce it if you can to bring about a smoother, more harmonious relationship, which increasingly gains these qualities to the extent it is based on trust.

Summary Chart

When To Put Your Own Anger Aside

- Your anger is feeding the other person's anger.
- The emotional intensity is escalating without effect.
- You have already let some of the anger out.
- It is necessary to work towards a future solution, rather than rehash the past.

How To Put Your Own Anger Aside

- Talk to yourself and tell yourself to stop.
- Use other self-calming techniques and let go.
- Propose that you both put your anger aside to deal with the problem.

When To Listen to Someone Else's Angers and Fears

- The other person has intense feelings about something and needs to vent them.
- The other person isn't willing to listen to you.
- The other person has feelings of hostility or suspicion that are creating an anger or distrust barrier to communication.

How To Respond to Someone Else's Angers and Fears

- Listen calmly to what the person has to say.
- Answer questions the other person has.
- Even if the other person raises questions or responds with an angry, hostile, suspicious tone, remind yourself to stay calm and respond neutrally yourself.
- Be prepared to be patient, show your willingness to listen, and be reassuring.

When To Let Go and Walk Away

- The build-up of anger and hostility is very great.

- You find you are obsessing about the situation—you keep dwelling on it, and when you do, you just feel more anger and frustration.
- The emotional frustrations and angers caused by the relationship aren't worth it.
- There are no major reasons you need to preserve the relationship.
- There seems to be no realistic way of resolving the problem or letting go of your anger or distrust.
- You want to move on.

How To Let Go and Walk Away

- Do a cost-benefits analysis which shows you the losses of continuing the relationship are greater than the benefits of continuing it.
- Realize it's time to cut any past losses and leave them behind.
- Remind yourself that the payoffs from the relationship are less than ending the relationship.
- Give yourself the permission to let go and walk away.
- Keep telling yourself it's over and it's time to move on.

3

Dealing With Your Own Anger and Fear in a Conflict

Feelings of anger and fear can build up easily in any conflict situation. These only fuel the conflict further. Previous chapters described the importance of letting others release their angry, negative feelings to clear the way towards a resolution. They also suggested that you'll need to let go of some of your *own* anger. But it's one thing to think about what you should do and another thing to actually release those negative emotions.

This chapter will teach you some visualization and other techniques for dealing with your own anger and fear. If a conflict with another person is worth resolving, you'll want to devote some of your energy to taking that person's needs and desires into consideration. You want to help that person feel better about the situation so you can patch up your relationship. But it is just as important that you take care of yourself. Of course you want to feel heard, and that your needs are being considered—but there are many things you can accomplish without relying on the other person. You can learn to control—and overcome—your own blocks to a successful resolution.

Releasing Anger

A critical step to solving any conflict and renewing a good relationship is letting go of anger—both yours and the other person's. Sometimes this means putting it aside, as when you make yourself listen to the other person's tirade for a bit. But ultimately you have to acknowledge your anger and deal with it more effectively. The trick is to learn how to release it with control.

The wrong way to release your anger is to attack or explode with it. An example of this might be the long-term relationship in which your feelings of anger have built up. You may want to keep blowing off steam at the other person. A typical instance of this might be the husband and wife or the boyfriend and girlfriend who have been together for years. They have a fight, and the anger escalates as one or both of them start bringing up everything the other person has ever done wrong in the past. This kind of attack does nothing to solve the immediate conflict—or defuse the anger. Everybody just gets upset and ends up screaming. You might have found yourself in a similar situation, and realized that only by calming down could you resolve the problem at hand. You probably also found that ignoring or denying your anger left you feeling as frustrated as when you screamed.

Fortunately, it *is* possible to silence your anger and take care of your frustration at the same time. This is usually an internal process. Work on it even as you listen to the other person vent—even scream—his or her built-up emotions. Then, ideally, you will both be ready to move past the anger (which you defused, and he or she vented) and settle down to deal with the conflict.

Letting Go of Your Anger

One approach to dealing with your own anger is to release it internally through visualization or a releasing ritual. This is especially effective when it isn't appropriate to vent anger to others, such as your boss, or when you realize that expressing your anger will only escalate an already volatile situation.

Basically, a visualization involves seeing yourself doing or experiencing something in your mind's eye, such as imagining that you are expressing the anger you feel towards a person. You achieve a feeling of release, but you don't get in trouble by expressing this openly. A releasing ritual involves a similar process, except that you act out your feelings in a private place. At times you need this kind of personal release so any unreleased anger can safely pass through you and be let go. There are a number of ways you can do this with visualizations or releasing rituals. The following are some possibilities. Choose those which feel most comfortable to you, or create your own.

Getting Rid of the Anger by Grounding It Out

In this technique, you visualize anger coming into you like a beam of negative energy from the person or situation that triggered it. But then, you imagine this energy moving downward within you and then dispersing harmlessly into the ground.

Getting Rid of the Anger by Projecting It Out and Eliminating It

Another way to get rid of anger is to get into a very relaxed state, and then imagine that you are sending out the anger within you and projecting it onto a screen. Next, imagine taking a ray-gun, and shooting that anger. (This takes care of your more violent urges!) Each time you zap it, you experience the anger releasing and draining away.

Cleansing Your Energy To Shake Off Your Anger

A third approach to get rid of anger or other negativity is to cleanse the energy field or aura around you. To do this, stand or sit up straight and rub your hands over your head, imagining that these gestures are clearing out the energy field around this part of your body. Then, as you do this, feel yourself drawing the angry or other negative feelings out of yourself, and then shake them off.

Releasing the Anger by Cutting the Person Who Makes You Angry Down To Size

You can also release your anger against a particular person by making that person seem smaller to you, so he or she is less important. This technique can be especially appropriate to use when you keep dwelling on that person, so he or she looms large in your life. You don't need to be in the middle of a particular conflict or even a discussion for this to work.

Begin by seeing yourself talking to this person. See him or her doing whatever it is that makes you angry—such as lying to you, not listening to you, acting like a know-it-all, or whatever. As you talk, watch this person shrinking in size. Notice the voice becoming fainter and fainter. Soon he or she should begin to seem *much* less important or powerful to you. Then, when you see yourself leaving this tiny person, you should feel very powerful yourself. Or if you prefer, you might imagine this person becoming so small that he becomes like a puddle, one you can step in or splash under your feet. So again, you have put this person in his place.

As with any of these techniques, you can repeat it if memories of the situation or the person come back. It may take some repetition if your anger about this situation has been building up for some time. But gradually, as you work with this release process, the anger and bitterness you feel will melt away. The person or situation might even seem funny to you.

Getting Rid of Your Anger by Learning From the Situation

Still another method of release is to look at the situation which has caused you to feel anger or other negative emotions and ask yourself: "What can I learn about dealing with future situations from this? How can I make sure I don't get stuck in this kind of problem again?"

This kind of approach can help you release, because it gives you some productive ways of dealing with what has happened. It also leads you to learn something—how better to deal with a negative situation in the future. You don't have to feel the conflict or situation was a waste of time and effort. Instead, you can see it as a chance to learn and grow, and in coming to this realization, you will feel a release of anger. For through learning, you have transformed your anger into something positive and productive.

Protecting Yourself From Negative People

Some people are just plain negative. If you find yourself around someone who is consistently angry, hostile, argumentative, critical, or otherwise troublesome to deal with, you'll need to set up some psychological barriers or protections against this person. These can be particularly useful if you have to be around someone who is negative on a day-to-day basis and you can't simply pull out and end the connection. (For example, you work together, or this is a relative who lives nearby.) But by closing yourself off, you can shut out the feelings of negativity you experience around this person.

It is important to do this, because being around such a person can really pull you down and may easily suck you into a conflict as a result of your bad mood. To prevent this, you can create a mental wall of energy around yourself to keep this negativity out. Whenever you feel threatened by this potential negativity, you put up the wall. You can be selective in when you do this, so your wall doesn't push away everyone—just the person or persons you feel are negative and thus threaten your own positive feelings.

One way to create this wall is to imagine a white light of pure, positive energy around yourself. Another is to see yourself in a protective bubble. Or even use the image of yourself as a duck, and see the negativity, like water, running off the back of this duck (you!). You can use many possible visualizations. The point is to use an image to create a zone of protection around yourself. Then, whenever you feel threatened by any negative energy from others, just put up your shield to ward it off or even send it back to the person from whom it comes. You'll feel more centered and grounded, and can more calmly and comfortably do whatever you need to do.

Learning To Let Go of Difficult Relationships

Another way to deal with conflicted, problem relationships is to let the relationship go when you can do so. If you find that a person is too negative or the relationship has been rocky for some time, think about whether you really need that relationship. If not, end it, and perhaps do a visualization of release to see it gone. Or perhaps just minimize your contact and find alternative things to do to replace being with that person. It may also be appropriate to let go of the relationship if you find that the other person is holding you back, because he or she might have a certain conception of who you are, although you see yourself differently or have changed. In fact, this particular problem often comes up when you go through a period of change or self-development, and the people you have been around aren't ready to accept your change. So, should this happen, you might need to let them go, or at least pull away for a time. Create a protective distance between you and the relationship. If you do have a need to make any contact, you might try a visualization as a way to help you keep your distance.

One woman who went through a series of personal development and spiritual growth programs found she had to create more distance between herself and her mother for a time. They continually argued and her mother had a very negative, grim way of looking at the world, so her mother's presence and point of view soon undermined this woman's own positive feelings after just a short time around her. The more sensitive and aware the woman became as she changed, the more deeply wounded she felt by her mother's negativity and the more she needed to disconect. She explained what happened:

> Ever since I have been young, I have had this war with my mother, because she has this very negative way of looking at everything. So she thinks that everything that can go wrong in your life will go wrong, and she thinks you're probably wrong if you make a decision.
>
> It became even more difficult to have a relationship with her as I started to become more sensitive. I increasingly found it difficult to be around her for more than about an hour or two, or I would start to feel irritable, depressed, and hostile. So I found I had to set up all these protections and barriers around myself to keep her negativity from affecting me, but after a while, it was such an effort to keep up this wall, and after perhaps two or three hours, I felt drained.
>
> I found it even more difficult to spend much time with her and take all this negativity heaped on me. So after a while, I gradually didn't see her very much. I found reasons why I couldn't come and visit, and I found ways to cut the visit short, when I did. And this approach helped me to feel much better. I felt like I had made something of

a break, though I couldn't do it completely. As a result, I felt much freer than ever before. It was like I had left her prison.

Likewise, if you can't resolve the conflict in a relationship, you may have to do this with people. You may have to break away.

Similarly, if you find that people in the business world are standing in the way of your success, even by having an attitude that puts you down (for instance, they deflate your confidence by suggesting you won't make it or they urge you not to think so big), then let them go.

In short, whatever you are doing, if you find yourself around a negative person who is putting or pulling you down, consider letting that relationship go, particularly if you have found the negativity so strong or continued that your efforts to put up mental protections simply don't work. Instead, it may be time to walk away—or if a total break isn't feasible, at least cut down the time you spend together. To whatever extent possible, cut this person out of your life and let go.

Learning Not To Take It Personally

Another strategy that can work effectively to avert conflicts and to feel better about backing down is to distance yourself from the situation. You can learn not to take a conflict personally. This allows you to side-step some problems and to feel good about yourself at the same time. It also clues you in to a truth: another person's negative or provoking behavior is often not directed specifically at you. The other person might have a problem; it has nothing to do with you, so why take it on?

This kind of approach can be particularly useful in casual encounters. You may come up against a person who is feeling angry about some existing situation. You just happen to appear on the scene and trigger the person's angry response. It's easy enough to respond with your own anger. It might be justified, but that's a sure way to begin—and keep building—a serious conflict. If you can learn to respond by not taking such anger personally, you may be able to pass the conflict by. You'll also do a service for your relationship with the other person (if you want to preserve it), and for your self-esteem.

One woman in a workshop described facing such a situation when she got on a bus. The bus driver snapped at her when she tried to give a man who seemed confused some information on where to go. As she explained:

> I told the bus driver that I was trying to help, because the driver hadn't responded to the man. But the driver was furious. He said the man had been on the bus before and he knew exactly where to drop the man off. I was wrong, and should just keep quiet.
>
> Then, as I was getting off the bus, I commented that I was just trying to be helpful. The bus driver came back in a surly tone: "Well, you gave the man the wrong information."

The woman felt like yelling back at the driver, although she said nothing. The incident made her upset for the next few hours. The driver's attitude had made her feel stupid and humiliated. "And I was just trying to help," she said.

In such a situation, it's appropriate to back off. The woman probably wouldn't want to end up in an argument with the bus driver over his nasty attitude towards her. That would only create a more heated confrontation. It would also be to no good end. She had nothing to gain from standing up to the bus driver, except perhaps salving her wounded pride. But that was something she could do for herself.

To do this, she might begin by realizing that the bus driver reacted as he did because he was already feeling tense and under pressure. Why? She might give herself some reasons such as: the people on the bus give him a hard time all day long; he has people asking him questions; people tell him again and again where to stop; and he has the pressure of traffic jams, drivers who cut him off, people who don't get out of the way when the light turns green, and so forth. So he feels tense and irritable, and he probably also feels a loss of power because of all these pressures. As a result, when a person starts giving information about where to get off to someone else, he might feel a threat to his own role. So he gets angry. And who knows, maybe there were other pressures at home or work that darkened his day.

Then, having considered these various possibilities, the woman could turn her attention back to herself without anxiety. She could realize she did nothing wrong; his response was his problem. In fact, not talking back to him was just the right thing to do. So by going through this process, the woman will become empowered, not demeaned, by the encounter. She just had to take the time to run over it in her head to convince herself of this.

The woman in the above example was lucky; she could just walk away. But the technique of depersonalization works even if you have to continue to deal with people or situations that make you feel bad. The key is learning to separate yourself from the problem so you feel it's outside of you. This will let you approach it in a neutral way. In most cases, you'll be able to avoid self-blame. You might even find positive ways to look at the experience: as a lesson for the future or a way to strengthen your own techniques of visualization and conflict management.

Of course, there is always a possibility in thinking honestly about a situation that you will decide you were *not* right. This requires detachment as well: first in realizing you were wrong, and then in deciding what to do about it. The advantage of this approach is that if a similar situation arises, you can perhaps be more flexible and objective about it in the future.

Take Some Mental Revenge

Sometimes nothing soothes anger as well as thoughts of revenge. Happily, you may be able to achieve the same end without resorting to violence—through mental revenge. Real revenge might not be a good strategy anyway; it would just escalate the conflict. On the other hand, if you imagine taking some action to punish or get back at whoever wronged you in your mind, you may feel better without endangering yourself— or others. However, it's important to emphasize that this is an approach that may work for some people but not others. With some people it serves as a useful release, but other people may find thinking these violent or angry thoughts increases frustration. So approach these techniques cautiously. If they seem to relieve the tension for you, fine. But if they only serve to refocus your anger and up your irritation level, then don't use these techniques.

Some people believe this mental processing can have a real physical effect, either by affecting how you relate to the person who wronged you, or by actually affecting the wrong-doer directly in some way. But leaving metaphysical results aside, the process of taking mental revenge may at least serve as a release if this technique works for you. The way it works is you direct your hostile feelings about the situation mentally out at the wrong-doer (instead of inward, toward yourself), so you feel a tremendous emotional release and liberation.

One woman did this when a neighbor clipped off the top of her tree which obscured his scenic view when she was on a vacation. When she got back and asked him about the missing limbs, he denied it. She had no proof. But convinced he had done it, she stewed about the problem for months, feeling further confrontations with him would be hopeless. Also, she was afraid of doing anything in retaliation. He might, after all, do something even worse to her. She was finally able to release this accumulated negative energy in a workshop by going into a relaxed state where she found a power animal who would help her deal with this neighbor. The animal was a gorilla, and in her mind, she saw the gorilla lumber over to the neighbor's property. There, he climbed up and tore the foliage off one of her neighbor's prize trees. Then he ripped up her neighbor's lawn and garden of plants before running off. The gorilla finally climbed her own battered tree and patted it with his hands, as if to heal it.

As a result of this visualization, the woman suddenly felt much better. She had let go of the built-up anger inside her, and her healing process could begin. This was symbolized by the image of the gorilla patting her own tree with healing energy. In fact, after the experience, the woman felt so much better that she actually approached her neighbor the next day on her return home from work. She told him firmly that she knew he had clipped her tree no matter what he claimed, and that he should stay off her property in the future—or else. Then, feeling fully restored and free of the anger of the past, at least for a while, she returned home. She felt she could put the problem out of her mind for a while. Although the problem with her neighbor did flare up again when the neighbor stopped by to complain about her tree several weeks later, the visualization gave her some temporary respite.

It's easy to learn how to take mental revenge to release your anger. You simply go through a visualization in which you imagine yourself or someone acting for you taking some action to appropriately punish the person who has wronged you. It's even fun to think of the appropriate revenge. You begin by entering a relaxed state. A dark room helps you tap into your intuitive, unconscious mind. So take a few deep breaths. Then, when you feel very relaxed, mentally ask yourself the question: What can I do to get a just punishment or revenge for _____. You fill in the blank with a capsule description of the situation. Afterwards, just observe what happens and see yourself getting and enjoying your revenge. Later, when you come back to normal consciousness, notice if you feel better about the whole thing. If you do feel in a better mood and feel less tension, then this is a good technique for you. But if not, if the anger is still there, then use a different anger-releasing or transforming approach.

You might also take some conscious, symbolic action to experience this revenge and release, again noting if this is an effective releasor for you. If so, use it. If not, don't. Some possible symbolic actions might be: write a nasty letter, but don't send it; plot out a scenario of the things you would like to do if you could do anything (such as embarrassing the person who insulted you publicly by having him parade naked down the street); or even ask a lawyer to write and send a letter, though you have no intention of taking any further legal action. Still another effective method for some people is to create a symbolic revenge ritual. You choose certain ritual words or paraphernalia to create a ritual setting to intensify your feelings and promote an altered state of consciousness. You might simply light candles, or you might draw the person's face to have him or her "present." The process is a little like throwing darts at the person's image on a dartboard. Then, in this relaxed ritual space, you imagine yourself obtaining the just punishment or revenge, much as in a relaxed meditative state. Here, though, the imagined experience may feel more intense, because of your actions to create and work in a ritual setting.

However you seek your revenge mentally (assuming this is an effective technique for you) it is important to seek only that revenge which you feel is just. This is what gives you a sense of putting things back into balance when you go through the process. After you finish with the visualization, conclude with a reminder to yourself that the situation is *over*. You have done what is necessary to obtain a just result by seeking this mental revenge, and now you can let it all go. It's all behind you, and you can go on to something new.

Overcoming Fears and Inner Conflicts in a Conflict Situation

Sometimes fears and inner conflicts prevent you from expressing what you really want to say or what you mean in a conflict situation. This will certainly make you feel frustrated, and probably, in the end, resentful. These negative emotions can lead easily to further miscommunication, and that will only make a conflict harder to resolve. Accordingly, just as you must learn to deal with your anger, you may need to confront these fears or inner conflicts.

These fears might be almost anything. A fear of failure might prevent you from asking an employer or associate for something you want, such as a raise or a chance to take on more responsibility. Then, because you don't get what you want, you may feel hostility or anger towards this person, and that poisons your future interactions. So you act with reserve, or perhaps you even try to justify your actions by telling yourself that this person is unfair, doesn't like you, is your enemy, or whatever. But underneath this apparent reality is the true, deeply buried reason for the disturbed relationship—your fear of failure. Not asking for what you want can lead you to relate to this person in ways that bring about the very failure you fear.

Or perhaps other fears cause you to hold back for other reasons such as a fear of ridicule, a fear of wasting time, a fear that you aren't as powerful as you should be, and so on. It doesn't matter what the particular fear is. The key to overcoming any fears is first to recognize them. Then, you need to decide if the fears are rational in light of the situation. Ideally, you'll be able to work on eliminating the fears, so you can act without fear and clear the way to a resolution.

Recognizing Your Fear Barriers

If you aren't clear what your fears might be in a conflict situation, one way to find out is to ask yourself through visualization. This allows you to tap into the fears that are not immediately evident to you. It is a powerful technique, because you can *see* how these fears stand in your way.

Begin simply by relaxing. Make sure you are comfortable—sitting or lying down is fine—and focus on your breathing. Breathe in and out deeply at least five times. You want to open yourself to an altered state of consciousness—like in a daydream. Slowly put up a screen in your mind and see the conflict you want to resolve on the screen before you. See yourself in the conflict; see the other players; and see some scenes in which the conflict occurs. The process is a little like watching different takes or scenes for a movie. Imagine the lights flickering, and see the fast cuts from one scene or frame to another. You are operating the projector and you can fast forward from one scene to another. You can experience a single scene or a collage of scenes about the conflict.

Allow yourself a few minutes for this, so your pictures come into focus, and you have a clear sense of what the conflict is about. Then ask yourself what fears are getting in the way of a resolution, and watch the screen for your answers. Don't try to answer this question logically. Try to be as passive and receptive as you can be. Wait for the answer to appear on the screen: you don't want to force it. This passive, receptive role frees your inner self or unconsciousness to speak to you. As many artists and writers have found, your unconscious commonly has the answer to a problem your conscious mind can't solve.

You may get this answer in the form of words, or it may come as a picture of your fear. You might even get your answer as more of a feeling. For example, if you feel a comfortable, warming glow, that might be a sign you are attracted to taking a particular action. On the other hand, if you feel a tightening pressure in your stomach, that could be a sign of resisting a particular event or person.

Determining If Your Fears Are Rational

You might be able to tell just by thinking about it whether the fear you have identified is a realistic one. It might be—but it might also result from a personal block, such as a lack of self-confidence or feelings of low self-esteem. For example, you might be resentful because you think your boss won't give you the promotion you feel you deserve. Is it *possible* that you're just feeling extra anxious because you want it so much? Could it be that you're afraid you won't measure up, and are projecting your self-doubts externally onto others, since they're easier to blame than yourself? Asking yourself these kinds of questions can bring an accurate answer to light. You might also try imagining someone in your place—or sending a letter to someone—describing the situation. What would you think? What would you tell yourself to do? It's easier to gain perspective when you see things from the outside. You might even be able to confide in someone else. What does a non-involved friend think?

However you arrive at your answer, and whichever it is—a real externally-based fear or a self-created one—you can now work on overcoming it. Say if you recognize, to take the earlier example, that your boss doesn't like you, think about what you can do to change this person's opinion of you so he or she won't stand in your way. Or if you realize you are generating the fear yourself because you have a lack of self-confidence, you can work on improving your self-esteem. You might work on something you have a good chance of achieving, to begin with. The solutions here aren't always easy or evident. But knowing where the problem lies enables you to direct your energy efficiently.

Eliminating Your Fears

Your goal, of course, is to get rid of the fears in your way. Once again, the visualization process can help you.

You'll need to get back into a relaxed state to get the most out of this exercise. Go back to your most comfortable position, and close your eyes. Breathe deeply in and out, and feel tension slip away. When you feel very relaxed and ready, put your screen back up—you might even see yourself in a theater this time. Now project an image of your fear onto the screen. Ask for a concrete picture, feeling, or words to appear to represent this fear. Once you get some response, ask yourself what is the *source* of the fear. Then wait for your response once more. Again, it may be in either pictures, feelings, or words.

Take a minute or so to see, hear, or experience this fear and its source on the screen before you. Notice the situations in which this fear arises—you might project several scenes onto your screen. Try to determine the ways in which your fear contributes to the conflict you have with this other person or persons.

Now ask what you can do to get rid of this fear. Again, don't try to answer the question consciously. Just let the answer somehow appear for you on the screen, and notice what it tells you to do. Maybe you'll find that relaxing and not worrying is the answer: just be patient and the thing you fear will go away. Or maybe you'll find you can follow a series of steps to get rid of the fear: you can take classes to learn the skills that will make you feel more comfortable and competent doing whatever you are doing.

Finally, conclude with the experience of the fear becoming smaller and vanishing. Use whatever image you like for this. You might see yourself shooting a laser gun at the fear image you have, so the fears you have explode in space. You might see the image of your fears grow smaller and smaller on the screen before you until they become just a point of light and finally vanish. You might imagine yourself grabbing your fear image like a piece of paper and tearing it up into little bits and then burning it. Or create some image of your own that makes you think of things ending or being destroyed.

Once you've achieved this feeling of completion that your fear is gone, come back slowly into your normal state of consciousness. You'll probably feel more powerful and more able to deal with your conflict situation. In some cases, a single visualization may be all you need. You identify the problem and eliminate it. But in other cases, you may find the fear has been unaffected, reduced a little, or only affected for a short time. This is perfectly natural. Your fear may have built up a long history, or you may hold onto it more intensely than you guessed; so it can take time to truly reduce or dislodge it. If this is the case, you may need to repeat this process from time to time for reinforcement. It's particularly helpful right before you encounter the person involved in the conflict with you. And, of course, be sure to follow any steps the visualization suggests to you, such as taking classes or being more assertive.

Another way to eliminate fears is simply to confront the fear head on and push right through it. To do so, you might try to force yourself to do something that frightens you, and experience and acknowledge the fear while you are doing it (such as asserting yourself to someone to say what you really want). In using this confrontation approach, it might work better to do this gradually; to confront the fear in a small dose (such as asserting yourself to a clerk in a store), and slowly work up to confronting something that seems more risky or scary to you (such as telling your boss what you want). This way you gradually increase the level of fear you experience and master each new level. This kind of approach has proved effective in treating people with all sorts of phobias.

You might also try combining this confrontation method with a visualization. To do so watch yourself go through the steps you need to take, and watch yourself succeed. If you are able to visualize this encounter, it is a strong message that your fear is unnecessary. Letting go of that fear becomes relatively easy. Perhaps you can just rationalize it away; or you can consider it *already gone*. You can always resort to more visualizations to destroy what remains: such as laser-zapping it, crumpling it up, or throwing it away. It may take some repetition to let go entirely, especially if the fear is a strong one that has become a habit. But each time you confront the fear (just as when you visualize it), it should take a little bit of the charge out. Ultimately, you will have neutralized it.

Affirm Your Fear Is Gone and Affirm Yourself for This Achievement

It is a noteworthy achievement to overcome the fears that hold you back. So be proud of your courage in trying to do this, and when you succeed, congratulate yourself.

You might even take a few minutes to visualize yourself fear-free, and getting a reward for it. Use the same process described earlier for getting into a relaxed state. Then, seeing the screen before you, see yourself engaging in some activity that shows the fear is gone. Say you used to be afraid of speaking openly to your boss; see yourself criticizing him or her with complete confidence. Then, see your boss responding thoughtfully and positively in response to your communication.

After experiencing your accomplishment, give yourself the reward. To do so, imagine yourself getting anything you would find rewarding. It could be a reward related to the particular situation you have overcome (your boss giving you a medal for calling attention to problems at work, plus a large bonus check); or it could be a more general type of reward (standing in front of a large cheering audience, receiving a plaque of recognition; going on a big, all expenses-paid vacation; sipping Pina Coladas under a palm tree).

Afterwards, return from this visualization feeling very good and proud about your accomplishments. You have overcome one more fear and eliminated one more barrier to resolving any conflicts in your life. You've also demonstrated strength and control over your thoughts and feelings.

Applying This Process to Other Negative Feelings

You can use the same methods for dealing with any other inner conflicts or negative feelings that might be contributing to a conflict situation. If you are feeling guilty about something, resentful, jealous, or whatever, begin by acknowledging that feeling. You then need to determine the *source* of the feeling and ask yourself if it is a rational response to the existing situation or if it is generated by your own misperceptions. To get through any outside conflicts, it helps to overcome your inner conflicts or negative feelings, no matter where they come from. Visualization can help you do this, and so can confronting your concerns by going through the situation in real life. Or perhaps a combination of visualization and confrontation will help—or try a more gradual confrontation approach where you gradual-ly up the fear level to confront things that are increasingly difficult for you. You might picture yourself in a situation where you have similar feelings in the past and are eliminating these feelings now. Once you succeed in overcoming a particular inner conflict or negative feeling, affirm this and acknowledge and reward yourself for this achievement. Recognizing that you have moved past one more barrier; so you are better able to deal with conflict situations in the future; and are ready to move on to higher levels of achievement, as well as better relationships with others and yourself.

Part II

Using Your Reason
To Understand
and
Manage Conflicts

4

The Responsibility Trap

Responsibility can play a role in conflict in a number of ways. Just as a person who fails to take responsibility can trigger a conflict, so can a person who takes on too much. And someone who tries to make someone else take on responsibility he or she doesn't want can trigger a conflict too. These extremes in taking or giving responsibility can produce conflict because of the reaction they produce in others. When one person fails to take responsibility, others can resent being left with the blame or the work; while when someone takes on too much responsibility for something, and perhaps too much of the credit, others can feel resentful or alienated. Then, too, no one likes being held responsible for something he or she didn't do.

Often such failures of giving away or taking on too much responsibility can occur because of mutual misunderstandings. This may happen when the parties involved think they are behaving appropriately from their own interpretation of the facts of the situation. But the other party is responding to their actions in different, unexpected ways because he or she has a different interpretation. So there can be a basis for a great deal of uproar when people with differing views accuse each other of not being responsible, or of taking too much control. When this happens, people have fallen into the responsibility trap. To get out, they have to either align their interpretations or bring the misunderstandings to the surface, so they can work to some compromise.

The Problem of Not Taking Responsibility: Feuding Neighbors

Mrs. Ortega wouldn't take responsibility for damages she caused her neighbors; she blamed them (and others) for the problem. Yet, since the problem was of her own making, she would eventually have to suffer even more severely than if she acknowledged her responsibility and worked with her neighbors to try to come up with a solution in the first place.

The problem began because of Mrs. Ortega's tree. It was a beautiful, old oak, but as it grew, its branches spread out. It ended up dropping leaves next door, and according to Mrs. Ortega's neighbor Mrs. Warren, the leaves had clogged up her drains. And the branches had poked a hole in her roof, so now the rains came in. Both women had lived in this quiet neighborhood for about 15 years. In the past, Mrs. Ortega had found a few of her tenants to trim the tree's branches. But now Mrs. Warren felt that Mrs. Ortega wasn't doing enough: she had already paid $1400 to fix her roof. Mrs. Ortega felt she had done what she could and there was no satisfying Mrs. Warren, apart from taking down the tree. She neither wanted, nor could afford, to do that.

When the two women showed up at a community resolution group meeting, the conflict had escalated to the "I'm ready to take this matter to court if you don't respond" stage. The two had already had one debate about the problem, which had resulted in a tentative resolution. It was obvious that this resolution was not holding together very well, and the tension level in the room was high.

"This has been going on for months like this," Mrs. Warren complained. "A few weeks ago Mrs. Ortega said she would check with her insurance company about the damages, and see about getting someone to take away the branches. None of this has happened." Mrs. Warren felt so frustrated as she spoke that she stood, ready to leave. She had been talked into coming to the meeting in the hopes that something could be done. But even before she arrived, she had expressed her doubts to the resolution group volunteer who set up the meeting. She had begun to feel that it was futile to deal with Mrs. Ortega anymore. "I've been to see my insurance company, and they say the damage to my house is definitely due to the tree. And now if Mrs. Ortega won't do anything, I'm ready to get a lawyer."

But Mrs. Ortega wasn't about to admit any of the tree damage was her own fault, regardless of what any insurance company or lawyer might say. She seemed most concerned with letting the volunteer panelists know she had done everything she could to help out, even though none of this was her fault. She had no money to pay for the tree problem anyway, she said. And besides, Mrs. Warren was just picking on her: because she was the only Hispanic person living on the block; because Mrs. Warren was using the tree as an excuse to get money from her to repair her own house, which was old; and because Mrs. Warren was a hard-to-please, picky person.

The debate went on and on. Mrs. Warren kept trying to bring the discussion back to Mrs. Ortega's responsibility for the tree and its damage. She mentioned her insurance company's verdict several times, and pointed out that she could get a lien on Mrs. Ortega's house if she got a judgment.

But Mrs. Ortega seemed to be in another world. She presented herself as a poor, misunderstood old woman who had no control over what had happened. Why pick on her? "I didn't plant the tree," she said.

It was there when I moved in. I don't know if the men who live in my house will do anything. They're just tenants, although I can ask them ... I don't see how the tree could have caused all the damage to her roof. Her house is old, and there would be damage anyway. She's just trying to get money from me to fix her house.... The other neighbors don't have any problem with the tree. They've never complained. Just Mrs. Warren.... She's very hard to please.... I did cut the branches in the past ... I've tried to be friendly with her, but she doesn't answer ... I think it's because I'm Spanish.... I've had some complaints about what the neighbors on the other side were doing, when they were watering their lawn too much, and it was flooding into my house.... But I never said anything to them. I didn't want to bother them and be unneighborly. So why should Mrs. Warren be so bothered by all this? If I was in her position, I would simply go and fix up my house myself. She certainly knows people who can do that. I wouldn't go out and bother my neighbor and get her involved.

In the middle of Mrs. Ortega's speech, Mrs. Warren stood up and started to leave. "This isn't getting anywhere," she announced. "I just better go ahead with my lawyer."

Before she made it out the door, some members of the community resolution group persuaded her to come back. "You've invested so much time in trying to deal with this. Just try a little bit longer."

Reluctantly she returned, and the group finally managed to hammer out an agreement. Mrs. Ortega agreed to do certain things, even though she never openly accepted her responsibility. She said she would ask the men in her house to trim the tree as soon as possible, and she would ask Legal Assistance to the Elderly if they might help her with some funds. In turn, Mrs. Warren was ready to accept the agreement. She would supervise the trimming, and if Mrs. Ortega couldn't get the funds from her insurance or legal aid, she would ask her insurance company if they might reimburse her.

It seemed like everything was settled: but then, on the verge of the two signing the agreement, it all broke down. One of the community panelists was reviewing what the two had agreed to when Mrs. Ortega began explaining once again why she wasn't responsible. She seemed willing to sign, but her words were angry.

"You know, she's still lying," she began. "Mrs. Warren just wants me to pay for fixing her house. She keeps saying my tree caused the damage, but it didn't. I don't care how many pieces of paper she waves. ..."

And with this Mrs. Warren walked out. The last outburst was just too much. She saw that Mrs. Ortega was still blaming her and not acknowledging her own responsibility for anything. Any agreement to act would be a fraud. If Mrs. Ortega wouldn't accept where her own responsibilities lay and acknowledge the damages she had caused, Mrs. Warren felt there was no basis for any agreement. As a result, Mrs. Ortega now faces almost certain judgment against her and a lien on—and possible sale of—her house, instead of a compromise solution with her neighbor involving minimal cost to her.

This situation illustrates one essential for resolving a conflict where responsibility is an issue. Each person *must* acknowledge any responsibility he or she has for something that has gone wrong. This can be hard to do, because it may mean the person has to make amends, do something to fix what is wrong, or pay for it. But if the person doesn't take responsibility, he or she is apt to pay even more in the long run. That person might also be subject to ongoing recriminations, including legal problems, that will make things worse, and could force him or her to take responsibility anyway. By contrast, if the person does accept responsibility for what he or she has done, he or she can do so in a way that saves face. This provides a basis for resolving a conflict: admitting to any deserved blame, if this is shown objectively to be the case.

Now, it isn't always necessary to assign blame to resolve a conflict. Sometimes the attempt to blame others—including the person who deserves the blame—can be fruitless and only fan the fires of conflict. That's the case in conflicts involving past wrongs that need to be put away so a relationship for the future can be preserved.

But when the conflict is the main issue in the relationship, or when one person needs to be compensated for damages suffered, then it is important for the person causing the damage to acknowledge it. Otherwise, as in Mrs. Warren's case, the person who suffered the damage can feel taken advantage of. A mutual agreement becomes almost impossible at that point. The standoff will only breed more hostility, and in the end the person causing the damage may have to pay more. An original refusal to accept a part in doing wrong both prolongs and intensifies a conflict.

If you find yourself in such a situation, and some of the responsibility for what happened is yours, acknowledge it. Let the other person know exactly what you did, from your perspective. This sets a tone of honesty and shows that you sincerely want to set things straight. It also allows you to apologize, if you feel that's appropriate. Or you can explain or justify your actions if the accusations against you seem hostile or unjust. You might admit you made a mistake, neglected to do something, or set the wrong priorities. In any case, the apology, explanation, or justification is a way of saving face by showing you are owning up to whatever happened.

At the same time, you don't want to appear too defensive or apologetic. That can feel demeaning for you, or actually antagonize the other person by creating an awkward, embarrassing situation. Your emphasis should be on speaking honestly about the situation and owning up to what you actually did or didn't do. In turn, the other person will generally be appreciative, since you are acting in a mature, responsible way.

If you are accused of something you feel you haven't done, try first to understand why you *seem* responsible. Is it possible you are more at fault than you first realized? Maybe, like Mrs. Ortega, you are trying to deny your responsibility—because you can't see the situation objectively, or because you fear the consequences of accepting responsibility.

Mrs. Ortega kept talking about all the efforts she had made to try to solve the tree problem, even though they didn't work out. She listed all the people she had called, although none of them had answers. She had worked hard, and felt that was enough to discharge any responsibility. But what she didn't realize was that her responsibility lay in producing *effective results* to resolve the problem. Spending ineffective time trying to achieve that wasn't enough. Mrs. Warren was quite reasonably holding her to this results-oriented measure. When Mrs. Ortega didn't accept this appropriate measure of responsibility—producing results, not just engaging in actions—Mrs. Warren only got madder and madder. It was one more sign that there was no basis for any agreement, since Mrs. Ortega continued to refuse her responsibility.

When you are accused of shirking responsibility, then take some time to look as closely and objectively as possible at your role in what happened. Maybe you do need to acknowledge responsibility, although you can do so in a comfortable, positive way (such as by explaining your reasons or your higher priorities). Also, you may need to *do* something about your error in order to work out a fair solution to the conflict. And if you aren't sure about your responsibility, you might respond with a hypothetical approach, such as: "Okay, let's say I am responsible. How do you feel we might work out the conflict?" See what sounds reasonable to you. Remember, it's better to resolve a conflict while you still have a say in it; don't let it get to the lawsuit stage.

But what if someone else is evading the responsibility, and you feel that person must accept blame if a fair solution is to be found? Bringing that thought to the person's attention in a gentle way is usually the best policy. Avoid sounding like you are accusing or blaming the person; you just want that person to recognize and take responsibility for a specific action or failure to act. An objective approach is best, but sometimes people resist seeing things that clearly. In that case, you still want to be direct. But use "I" statements instead of "you" statements in calling attention to what you see (see Chapter 6 for a description). For instance, Mrs. Warren had been telling Mrs. Ortega repeatedly that her tree was causing damage and that she was responsible for doing something about it. When that didn't work, Mrs. Warren might have confronted her neighbor's failure directly by saying something like:

> I feel like you are not willing to recognize that you are responsible for this tree. I feel like you are trying not to recognize this, because you are concerned about the financial costs of this responsibility. I'd like to try to work something out to deal with this problem without having to go to court. But the only way I can see to do this is if you understand that you have some responsibility for this. Then we could work on resolving the problem together.

These statements get the real issue on the table: a person's resistance to working out a fair solution. Once you can work on this, you'll have a basis for resolving the problem. If not, you may end up going round and round like Mrs. Ortega and Mrs. Warren; Mrs. Warren never directly raised the failure-to-take-responsibility issue, and Mrs. Ortega never realized that Mrs. Warren understood her reluctance to acknowledge responsibility.

The Problem of Taking too Much Responsibility: A Mother and a Daughter

Alas, the opposite problem is as great a source of conflict: when someone takes on too much responsibility, or tries to, others can feel put down and put upon. In effect, the person taking on extra responsibility exerts power over the person giving up responsibility. Especially when the person giving up responsibility does so reluctantly or unwillingly, he or she is likely to feel lowered self-esteem and some measure of resentment against the person wielding power. These feelings of hostility might simmer under the surface; but they can readily erupt into conflict when a situation occurs that fans the flames.

The person taking on the extra responsibility can feel put upon and resentful, too. Greater responsibility can be an unwanted burden. Someone might feel driven to take on responsibility if it seems the other person won't take it, or won't take it competently. Or perhaps one person wants the power and control that comes with being in charge, but doesn't like the additional commitment of time, energy, and effort required to exercise that added responsibility.

So both parties start to suffer when responsibility is delegated unevenly. Still, it's a pattern people sometimes fall into—another version of the responsibility trap. One reason the problem of taking too much responsibility can blow up is that while the responsible person may appear to be in control, the other party may feel resentful, frustrated, and tense. It's a pattern that can readily occur because it typifies one of the most basic human relationships—that between the parent and child. But when adults are involved, the person pushed into the "child" role by the person trying to act like the responsible "parent" may not like this and may seethe inside or eventually rebel.

The Parent-Child Pattern

It's natural for a parent to do things, give advice, and make decisions for a child. In the beginning, after all, a child relies on the parent for guidance and protection. But as children grow, so does their need to assume some of their *own* responsibility and direction. Some parents can find it hard to recognize and act on this. So a child's anger, confusion, or resentment can grow because the child wants to take on more responsibility, but the parents won't give that up.

Angie and her mother developed just such a problem. It began when Angie was still a young child, and it got worse as she grew up. Mother and daughter had frequent screaming battles, separated by uneasy truces until the next battle erupted. The problem, from Angie's perspective, was that her mother said "You can't [or won't] do this" to most things Angie felt able and eager to do.

As Angie commented, at a workshop, in thinking back to those tumultuous times:

> My mother always wanted to be in charge and tell me what to do, and I resented it. I felt like she was continuing to treat me like a child. She didn't trust me to grow up. Even when I was 17 and 18 she would do this.
>
> When we went someplace, she would tell me what to wear. If I wanted to choose something I liked, she would argue that I didn't look right, or that I was trying to wear it to displease her.
>
> She was also continually reminding me to do things I already planned to do, like go to an appointment in school or with a doctor. If I tried to tell her she didn't need to remind me, that I could think of these things myself, she would tell me she was just trying to be helpful. And sometimes she would say she felt she needed to do this, because I didn't always remember these things. She thought I couldn't be responsible, but she never gave me the chance to prove I could be.
>
> She was always giving me advice about things when I didn't want her advice. If I said I didn't want it, she would say it was for my own good, that I didn't listen, that this was one of my faults. She would tell me what she thought about my friends; she would tell me when to do the laundry and how to do it; she would tell me what she thought of my hair and what I should do with it.
>
> Most of the time, I did what she said just to keep the peace. But I kept steaming inside, because I felt she was trying to take over my life. She would push one of my buttons, and I would just explode. It didn't have to be a big thing—even just a piece of advice about how I should wear my hair or what clothes I should buy would do it. And then I'd start screaming at her, "no, just leave me alone," and she would scream back, "you don't appreciate all I'm trying to do for you." And I would say "I just want you to get off my case," and, of course, that would make

her even madder. It often ended with me storming off and slamming my door, or sometimes I got so tired of all the yelling that I just gave in. Sometimes my mother just backed off saying something like: "Oh, do what you want. I don't know what I've done to deserve this."

However it ended, I usually felt bad. There would be this tension between my mother and me that would simmer for days, until we ended up having some battle again.

These tensions and battles upset Angie's mother, Alice, too. But she kept on pushing: because she was genuinely concerned that her daughter would fare less well without her guidance, and perhaps because her own feelings of low self-esteem led her to want to feel this control over the situation. It was clear that Angie was resisting and resenting Alice's advice, but Alice found she couldn't help it. She felt driven to speak her mind, and couldn't control herself even when she realized that certain comments were likely to set Angie off. She felt it was worth the risk of an argument to keep her daughter's life on track.

Alice dreamt of a loving and warm mother-daughter relationship, even as her actions were driving Angie away. If asked, she would have said she *wanted* to give more responsibility to her daughter, but simply didn't feel she *could*.

In fact, Alice had mixed feelings about taking on all of this responsibility, due to her own insecurities and fears. On the one hand, she *did* want the added responsibility of controlling another person's life. She felt if she didn't have this control she would be diminished as a person, since she didn't feel fulfilled in her work or in other areas of her life. Staying in control of her child was a way she could give herself an anchor and a cause. On the other hand, she recognized the personal *costs* of taking on so much added responsibility. She felt under continual stress because she kept having to fight to maintain her control. There was also always the possibility of an eruption with Angie, and she hated to fight with the daughter she loved. Moreover, she hated the feeling she brought on herself by taking on all this responsibility: the feeling that it was her fault if things went wrong.

The first part of the solution was a long, hard, objective look at the situation. It was clear things couldn't go on as they had:

mother and daughter hardly spoke to each other without fighting. And to Alice it was clear that *she* had to change something; her need to control everything worked, for once, to benefit the relationship at this point.

And so—with the help of some outside advice and a visualization technique to envision a possible future—she decided to take a risk. She let Angie make all the arrangements for a day in the city with some visiting relatives. It was something both Angie and Alice had dreaded, only because they were sure to fight about it. Angie was actually looking forward to seeing cousins her age. However, she shuddered to think of the plans her mother would make for them and showing them her favorite parts of town; and the clothes she'd "suggest" she wear. But then she was shocked to hear her mother suggest Angie take charge of the plans. At first she was even nervous—she knew she could do it well, but it was something new. (And what was her mother thinking of, she wondered.)

Alice was nervous too—what if something went wrong? But she told herself it was a test. Maybe Angie couldn't handle the responsibility. Nothing was really lost, except one day, and she would appreciate her mother's input in the future. And maybe, just maybe, she would do fine on her own. At the least, Angie would be surprised and pleased to get her way.

The day in the city worked out wonderfully, thanks to some hard work on everyone's part (Angie to plan well, and Alice to hold back). Mother and daughter even had a long, honest talk afterwards. Alice acknowledged Angie's success and agreed to give her more space to run her life in the future. It wasn't easy for her. The process of giving up took a long time. She had become so used to her controlling mode of behavior. But with the help of counseling, Alice was able to work things out. She learned to hold back her desire to take on responsibility immediately, give advice, and exercise control. She was there if her daughter needed her, but she tried to stand back. She learned to let go, and the result was an immediate easing of tensions with her daughter. Soon Alice felt a sense of peace and harmony for herself. She was proud of the improved relationship she had worked out with Angie, and proud that the daughter she had raised *could* be so responsible. Angie made some poor choices every now and then, but she was allowed to learn from her errors, as most people do to grow further. And Alice replaced her need to take control over those who didn't want it with the act of taking on responsibility in volunteer activities, where people really did appreciate her efforts and were delighted when she assumed the responsibility she took.

Other Common Situations Involving Responsibility Issues

The parent-child relationship is one in which responsibility is both difficult and crucial to balance, but it is not the only such relationship. Any situation where one person takes on too much responsibility can lead to conflicts. These troubled relationships fall into typical patterns.

In one common situation, a person takes on extra responsibility because he or she doesn't think the other person is taking on enough. The other person is often unaware of the need for that responsibility. That person might also have different priorities, or might not see what has to be done since it *is* being done by the first person.

This is a frequent source of conflict between husband and wife. The wife might think the husband should do certain tasks around the house; the husband doesn't take on these responsibilities—such as making repairs or cleaning up—because he is busy doing other things, or he says he'll get around to them later, or he has a different standard of neatness so he doesn't think performing these tasks is necessary. A classic outcome of this kind of standoff is that the party who wants certain tasks done, the wife in this case, will do them, but feel resentful. Or she'll nag her husband about doing them, because she feels he *should* do them. In either case, both parties will feel burdened by what seems like needless responsibility. The wife will resent doing the task or having to nag and plead and demand, and the husband will resent time spent inconveniently (or unnecessarily) doing the task, or being made to feel bad about not doing it.

A related problem can occur in an office setting between co-workers involved in a joint project. One may begin to take over, to the other's dismay, and sometimes he or she may not really want to do this anyway—but does, feeling some need or pull to step in. He or she might act because he or she has certain ideas about how to do the project, or might not think the other can or will carry it out as well And as that person takes the lead, he or she may resent the co-worker for not doing enough. The co-worker, meanwhile, may feel shut out of the process, having lost control over it. And he or she is likely to resent the other person, too, for pressing ahead.

A key problem in these situations is that the person taking on the extra responsibility may truly be able to accomplish the goal more efficiently alone, or by directing both people's actions. But the costs of such an action are likely to outweigh the benefits. Feelings of anger and resentment can simmer or erupt on both sides. The person taking on the responsibility can feel burdened by the extra work and feel alone. Meanwhile, the person turning over the responsibility can feel a lowered sense of self-esteem and worth, as well as an uncomfortable dependence and a loss of individuality. Also, hostile feelings may readily expand into full-blown conflict. And even if such feelings remain under the surface, unshared, their toll in stress, anger, suspicion, and paranoia can be high.

Getting Out of the Responsibility Trap

You can fall into the responsibility trap from different angles, and land on different sides of it. One side is a perceived problem with *you*: you seem to be taking on too much responsibility, or not as much as others would like. The other side is a perceived problem with another person: that person seems to you to be taking too much control over a situation, or not taking as much as he or she should. It's true that opposite sides will overlap (you'll take on too much responsibility if the other person leaves too much up to you), but the key to resolving the problem is to figure out how most appropriately and comfortably to reapportion the responsibility. You want to resolve the problem for the future, regardless of who is currently to blame for taking on or not taking on enough responsibility in the past. The matrix of the responsibility trap will look something like this:

Amount of Responsibility Assumed

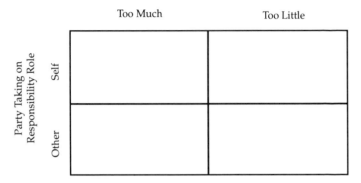

The first step to getting out of the trap is looking more closely at the situation. You might have developed strong feelings about who's at fault and who isn't, particularly if the conflict has become a recurring pattern. But now is the time to check out the accuracy of your perceptions, or to consider the other's view of you. You also need to consider possible reasons for either side to take on, or avoid, certain responsibilities.

One way to check the accuracy of each other's perceptions might be for each of you to share your view of the situation. Since this sharing could raise some tensions, it's a good idea to preface this sharing with an agreement that you will each listen to the other with respect and attention, even though you might each hear things you don't agree with. Then, after one person has finished, the other can respond by correcting or verifying any perceptions, and might provide some explanation for why such and such occurred. Another possibility might be for you both to engage in a role play in which you each imagine what the situation may have looked like from the other's eyes. Alternatively, if feelings are still too tense for direct discussion or role play to seem useful, you might suggest that each of you put your feelings and perceptions of the situation in a letter to each other. Then, after you both review these letters, you can meet to have a discussion. The process of writing such letters can help to clarify issues and provide explanations. This writing can also do much to release feelings and calm everyone down to pave the way for a fruitful discussion and an exchange of views.

Whatever you decide to do at any time in the process, if you realize you were doing or denying something that contributed to the conflict, acknowledge that to yourself. You need this initial self-awareness to decide how to deal with the situation. You may also want to acknowledge this to the other person to show your good faith in taking on responsibility where it's due.

For example, suppose you have been in a conflict with a significant other or co-worker who blames you for not doing certain tasks. You have been getting more and more angry at that person for bugging you about this. If it's so important to him, you think, why doesn't he do it himself? But he thinks you should do it, and so the conflict continues.

To start dealing with the situation, look first at what the person is claiming about you. Could it be accurate? If absolutely not, it might be helpful to correct faulty assumptions. Or the claims may be misplaced because of a lack of clarity about who should do what in the situation. Now is the time to discuss roles and responsibilities openly. Alternatively, if the person's perception might be accurate, think about why you might be avoiding that particular responsibility. Maybe you don't like doing this task; don't think it is necessary; have different ideas about the value of that activity; feel the other person isn't doing enough in other areas; feel you should get more pay or recognition for doing more; or whatever. The point is to understand what is causing the other person to view your actions in a certain way. Are your actions or your perceptions at fault, or are the other person's perceptions? And why are you choosing to act as you do in taking on or avoiding certain responsibilities? You'll need to work out these understandings before you can decide the best way for you to deal with the conflict.

You may decide that taking on the role the other person wants you to perform isn't such a big deal for you, and that you're willing to give in and do more. (This is an example of accommodating, as discussed in Chapter 7.) Or you may want to stand up for what you are doing and get the other person to back down, if you feel the other person is making unfair claims on your time. This usually requires a more competitive style of resolving the conflict (also described in Chapter 7). Or perhaps you might suggest a compromise where you take on more responsibility in this area to please the other, but ask that person to do something you want in return. Finally, if it's worth the time and effort to discuss the situation in depth, you might be able to collaborate with the other party to find an alternative solution. The idea is to base your approach on your most important goals and priorities, based on a clear appraisal of the situation.

Conversely, if you are in a situation where you feel the other person isn't doing enough, start by considering whether your own perceptions are accurate. Can you think of any reasons he or she might have to avoid this responsibility? These considerations will give you some basis for proposing or discussing a possible solution. For example, if an associate hasn't been doing something, and you have been nagging him to do it, you might write a list of possible explanations for his behavior: he doesn't like it; doesn't think he can do it well; feels you should do it yourself; or doesn't find it worthy of his time and attention. Then, you can consider which of these explanations is most likely in terms of his personality and past behavior. Once that's clear in your mind, you'll be able to tailor a discussion to address *his* needs as well as your own. Be sure to treat your assessment as an educated, reasoned guess. You still have to check out through a discussion of the other person's reactions what is correct. Before you move to bring the subject up again, though, you should consider how important this particular responsibility is for you. It may be that you'd as readily perform the action yourself. If not, a clearer awareness of your needs and your associate's needs might allow you to work out an agreement for the other to do it, in return for a compromise offer from you. If the task doesn't seem important to him, for instance, you might assure him it is to *you*, and offer to do something he values in return. For example:

If your roommate will agree to turn off the stereo at 10 p.m....	You will agree to be quiet in the morning and you will take your usual shower later in the day.
If your employee will come in over the weekend to do an extra unexpected project....	You will let your employee take off an extra Friday to have a long weekend anytime next month.

| If your spouse will agree to walk the dogs in the morning and at night.... | You will go to that luncheon with your spouse, though you really would rather not do it. |

The same process of analysis can be used to see you through a situation where one person is taking on too much responsibility and denying the other person power. Ask yourself whether either of you really is doing too much. Consider the possible reasons causing this: you don't trust the other person to do it right or he doesn't trust you; you want to prove your worth by showing how much you can do, or the other person is seeking such validation; one of you likes the feeling of power and control; and so forth. Which possibility sounds most plausible to you? You can assess your own and the other person's likely priorities based on your answer, and that should suggest ways of resolving the conflict.

For example, if you realize you *are* doing too much and are undermining the other person's self-esteem (resulting in hostility and resentment), maybe it's time to do a little less and let go. You might discuss exactly what the other person needs to do so you will feel comfortable letting go a bit. This way if you agree to give away some responsibility, you can make it clear that you need to feel the other person will act responsibly in return. Then if the other person agrees, be sure to allow him the space to do so. Alternatively, maybe the person needs to be acknowledged and supported in other ways, and you can continue doing what you are doing. Perhaps verbal praise and recognition for roles already filled is enough. Or maybe you need to do more, such as show the person some techniques so he knows what to do. It all depends on the situation and the needs, interests, and priorities you each bring to the situation.

If the other person is taking on too much responsibility from your point of view, use the same process in reverse. Start by examining the reality of your perceptions, and imagine *why* the other person might be doing this. Then, act accordingly. For instance, if doing so much is really important to the other person, you might work on calming and relaxing yourself, so his actions don't make you so resentful. Allow yourself to let go if you can, and if it's worth keeping the peace. Or you might offer to do more yourself. For example, suggest that you could do some task because you know the person is very busy, and this could give him more free time. Point out that you would really like to learn how to do something, so you can do it well. Maybe write up a note with your suggestions on how a particular task might be done and what you can contribute—an especially good approach in a work situation if you have an insecure boss who is afraid to give up responsibility because he isn't sure the employees are up to it. Again, the particular approach depends on the circumstances and what you and the other person most want.

The responsibility trap can cause a great deal of tension between people when they have different ideas about who should do what and have different priorities about what they want to do themselves. The way to get out of the trap is to look more closely at your own and the other's perceptions, priorities, and rationales for acting more or less responsibly. Based on what you find and the importance of the issue to you and the other party involved, you can choose your solution: find ways to step away from the situation; relax or accommodate yourself to what the other party wants to do; work out a compromise; deal with the problem at length to find a joint solution; or even continue doing what you are doing, while finding a way to make the other person feel better about the situation. This chart can help you in deciding what kind of approach to use.

Understanding the Responsibility Trap and Figuring How to Get Out

What is the problem?   You claim the *other party* is taking:

		Too Little Responsibility	Too Much Responsibility
The other party claims *you* are taking:	Too Little Responsibility	Conflict over one person doing too much when or because the other is doing too little	Conflict over having control
	Too Much Responsibility	Conflict over no one doing the job	Conflict over one person doing too much when or because the other is doing too little.

Then, for each claim or accusation consider:

1) Is it true?

2a) If so why? What are the reasons? (i.e.: lack of trust, the matter isn't important enough)

2b) If not, why? Are there incorrect perceptions? Are there wrong assumptions? Different priorities?

3a) What can you do to straighten things out: i.e., a lack of trust— build trust; not important enough—let the other person do it ; too important to risk not doing it—do it myself

3b) What can you do to straighten things out? i.e., incorrect perceptions—correct wrong perceptions; incorrect assumptions—bring errors into open and correct them; different priorities—work out compromises, so both can achieve highest priorities

It's easy to fall into the responsibility trap, and it requires conscious effort to climb out. But once you make the effort, you'll find you'll be more wary of such traps in the future. You'll recognize early the danger signs of someone taking too little or too much responsibility, and you'll keep yourself out of the trap by keeping responsibilities more evenly balanced, or working out agreements so people feel comfortable with an uneven split. Also, you'll avert potential conflict situations before they reach full pitch.

5

Recognizing the Reasons for a Conflict and Responding to Underlying Needs

Conflicts often arise when people have underlying needs or strong wants that aren't being met, such as a desire for security, perhaps independence, or belonging. Conflicts also grow out of fears that something valuable may be lost: a friendship, property, peace and quiet. On the surface, a conflict may appear unrelated to these needs. But unless these basic needs and wants are identified and dealt with, the conflict will probably continue, along with growing frustrations, unless the situation causing the conflict changes for other reasons (i.e., the person with whom you are in conflict leaves).

Sometimes underlying needs are expressed through strongly held, seemingly unchangeable positions. Picture, as an example, two long-term employees equally determined to get a higher position in the company. This can lead to an explosion of hostility that threatens the productivity of the company. And sometimes these needs and wants dictate a person's reaction (or overreaction) to a situation. You might greet someone with a harmless remark like: "Hi'ya Joe, what's new on the job?" only to unleash a wave of anger. Would you guess that Joe just had a fight with the boss and lost his job? You won't always have full information about all the issues in any encounter or conflict. But you can learn how to uncover what's really going on. The key is to recognize that true needs and fears often lie below the surface; if you can identify them—in yourself or the other person—you're on your way to a truly satisfying resolution.

Unfortunately, it may not always be obvious from the way a person acts or the position he takes in a conflict what those needs or fears are. People don't always want to reveal their true feelings. They might feel exposed or vulnerable, or worry that their true feelings will seem ignoble or be misunderstood. Sometimes people aren't even aware of their true feelings—they just think they want or need something, and seek it without really understanding why. If they had a sense of their true motivation, they might look for—or be willing to accept— something else.

Hidden needs and agendas keep the conflict pot stirred. The husband fights with his wife because he doesn't want her to go out to work, claiming it would harm their young child, when his real reason is a fear that her independence and skill would threaten his own competence. In response, she gets frustrated and resentful, instead of being able to address his fears while meeting her own needs. In another common situation, neighbors battle over issues of noise and garbage, when the real issue is fears and misunderstandings about differences in lifestyles. Or consider the office where an employee feuds with his co-workers and tries to undercut them to his employer, claiming they are doing poor work, when in fact he is worried about his own competence and feelings of low self-esteem. He tears down others in order to bolster up himself. You can surely think of examples from your own experience of how unspoken needs and wants contribute to conflict.

This is a key point in Roger Fisher and William Ury's popular book, *Getting to Yes*. They point out that many conflicts occur because people get stuck in positions and then focus on upholding those positions, instead of recognizing their underlying needs or interests which lead them to adopt that position. So their wrong focus stands in their way of finding a solution which depends on reconciling the underlying interests or needs of the parties involved. As they point out: "Reconciling interests rather than positions works for two reasons. First, for every interest there usually exist several possible positions that coud satisfy it. All too often people simply adopt the most obvious position ... (But) when you do look behind opposed positions for the motivating interests, you can often find an alternative position which meets not only your interests but theirs as well." Fisher and Ury suggest that reconciling interests can work better than trying to compromise opposing positions, because "behind opposed positions lie shared and compatible interests, as well as conflicting ones." (p. 43). Thus, it can be possible to achieve a resolution by discovering the ways in which underlying needs are compatible or shared.

If you can sense what those needs or fears *are* in others or in yourself, you can take them into consideration in working towards an effective resolution. You might seek to bring them out in the open to discuss them. Even if such a discussion is not feasible, you can still act in light of your perception of what those needs might be to satisfy the other person. Either way, you've taken a crucial step towards conflict resolution. In fact, by responding to the other person's true needs, you can develop a stronger, closer, more mutually satisfying relationship as a result.

This doesn't mean you should ignore your own needs in responding to the other person's needs. There may be times when you find the other person's needs are so much stronger than yours that you need to put your own needs aside—at least for a time—to focus on helping that person work through the conflict. When the immediate conflict is over with, you may find that your willingness to cater to the other person's needs are handsomely paid off in the other person's feelings of gratitude to you. There may also be times when the other person is in a more powerful position than you, or times when you feel you have more to gain out of the relationship than the other person does. These are pragmatic reasons to want to put the other's needs first. Ideally, you'll be able to come up with creative solutions that satisfy both of your needs. It just might mean addressing the other person's needs first, or more vocally, since he or she seems so needy at the time.

Alternatively, you might need to spend some initial time looking at your *own* real needs and fears before trying to settle a conflict, since this might lead you to finding alternative ways to get these needs met or your fears overcome. The two hostile employees locked in a struggle for a single position might have benefited from such an approach. Suppose, as one of those employees, you realized that your real reason for wanting that position was a desire for more prestige and more money. In truth, however, you realize that you would rather not take on the extra responsibility and time commitment that comes with the new position. You could then shift gears to go after what you really wanted—an enhancement in your current position, perhaps. The basis for the ongoing conflict with the other employee would fade away, and you might both end up with what you really want.

Thus, a key to achieving a resolution that works for everyone is to recognize those underlying needs or fears—the other person's or your own. Such recognition allows you to find responses that satisfy these needs or assuage these fears in order to resolve the problem. The following examples illustrate how effective this process can be, if you only uncover these needs and fears and respond to them appropriately.

Recognizing Needs and Fears

A good example of how it's possible to resolve a crisis by tuning into another person's needs and fears is illustrated by the case of Andrea M. Andrea had a powerful need for belonging and a fear of being alone. She also feared being taken advantage of. These feelings triggered a crisis in her relationship with Paula, who was acting as she usually did with other casual friends. Paula was initially unaware of Andrea's needs, and so was unable to respond to them. Only after she became sensitive to Andrea's feelings were the friends able to regain a rewarding relationship.

The problem started when Andrea returned to San Francisco after being out of town for almost seven months, trying to set up a therapy- healing practice. She was already feeling lonely and afraid, because she had met a number of rebuffs in getting her practice going. She was further disheartened by the impersonal way she noticed that people routinely treated each other. Other people suddenly struck her as manipulative and hard to trust. She noticed that many people seemed to come around her because they wanted to take advantage of her knowledge of healing practices. "They wanted to bask in my energy," she said. "They saw me giving workshops and gaining popularity, so they wanted to hang around. But after the first few workshops, when I continued to need some of their help in getting settled, I suddenly found they weren't so helpful and supportive. I would ask them for something, and they wouldn't be there for me. They might promise to do something, but not come through. Or they suddenly would claim to be busy, so they couldn't promise anything at all."

After seven months of this, Andrea felt it was time to move on. She stopped in San Francisco for a few weeks of workshops and individual counseling which she had arranged through some friends in the area. One of the people she called was Paula, whom she had met only briefly. But at the time, both of them felt there could be much for both to gain if they were able to work together. Paula suggested they team up to do a series of national programs and employ a single coordinator to set up arrangements for them both. It would be a perfect match, she said, since Paula specialized in more mental therapeutic approaches, while Andrea concentrated on more physical and emotional methods.

So when Andrea called announcing her arrival, Paula was delighted to have a chance to get together. She suggested that, since Andrea was there over the Thanksgiving holidays, Andrea might want to join her for a unique Thanksgiving dinner she was already going to. It sounded like the perfect way to renew their friendship. Andrea was especially enthusiastic because her only other option for Thanksgiving was a dinner with the family of the woman she was staying with on her visit. She felt she would have little in common with them.

But soon after they arrived at the dinner, everything seemed to fall apart. At first, Paula couldn't understand why. The afternoon began calmly enough. Paula asked Andrea to meet her at her house, since the dinner was being held in a church only a half mile away and Andrea was staying across town. "No problem," Andrea had told her and she took a taxi over. Then, as Andrea described how easy it was to find a taxi, Paula escorted her on a tour of her house, so Andrea could get a better idea of the kind of work she did. So far so good. Though they hadn't known each other very well before, Paula felt Andrea was very receptive to her own work, and she spoke of how they might talk more about ways of working together later.

Then, they headed for the dinner in Paula's car. Since it was just starting to rain, Paula took her umbrella. At the time, Paula didn't think anything about the rain as part of the problem. She parked about two blocks away from the church, and just wanted to get there as quickly as possible. So she walked quickly, holding the umbrella. Meanwhile, Andrea walked along a step or two behind. "Don't you want to get in under the umbrella?" Paula asked a few times. But Andrea didn't say anything and kept on walking a few paces behind; so Paula kept on going, and in a few minutes they were at the church.

Inside, a woman was at a table taking payments, and as Paula and Andrea had agreed in advance, they each paid for their own dinners separately. Paula paid first, and then as Andrea paid, Paula walked ahead to look for seats for them. Nothing unusual about that, she thought. She had done the same thing with other friends when they went to movies or other events, and they appreciated her going ahead to take care of such arrangements.

Unfortunately, Andrea perceived Paula's actions quite differently. The large impersonal setting of the dinner disturbed her, and it combined with her feelings of loneliness and alienation to trigger a crisis in their relationship. Andrea's upset was so severe, that what happened could have ended their possible collaboration and entire friendship that night.

The setting itself was a key part of her reaction. It wasn't what either she or Paula had expected. Instead of finding a warm, informal type of setting, which encouraged sharing and friendship, the two women confronted a large church auditorium which was set up with two rows of covered benches with chairs lined up around them, and tables for serving lined up along the side. The place looked a little like a charity soup kitchen. It was already crowded by people waiting at the tables, and there were few available pairs of seats remaining.

When Paula opened the door to this room and surveyed the

scene, she pushed back her own feeling of dismay and rushed in to secure neighboring seats for herself and Andrea. As soon as she did, she looked towards the door to see if Andrea was there yet. When she saw her standing there, she waved Andrea to come over.

But Andrea didn't appear to see her. Instead, Paula suddenly saw Andrea turn and close the door. "She's probably just looking for a ladies' room," Paula thought, and proceeded to watch the door and wait. However, after about 10 minutes, when Andrea didn't return Paula went looking for her. She discovered that Andrea had left the dinner entirely. "She suddenly said, 'I can't stay,' then she left," the woman who took the money at the door told Paula.

Paula was perplexed, and thought maybe Andrea's leaving had something to do with the place looking like a soup kitchen. She had no idea that she herself had done anything that might have contributed to the problem, and so she just found a phone at the church and left a message on the answering machine where Andrea was staying, letting her know how they could get together later after the dinner. But when Paula returned home after the disappointing dinner, she found a cryptic message on her tape from Andrea. "You can just leave the shoes I left in the car at my friend's house." Also, Andrea left a name and an address, but nothing about getting together later that night or during the few days that she would be in town.

Paula was completely baffled and called to find out what happened. Andrea seemed very cool and distant. "I felt so alienated and alone," Andrea said.

At first, Paula thought Andrea just meant she was put off by the dinner. "Yes, I know. It wasn't a very good dinner," she started to say. But then, she heard Andrea allude subtly to something else. "You were so far ahead of me. I felt abandoned."

It would have been easy to push these comments aside. Paula even started to do so by explaining rationally why she had gone ahead. "Oh, no. I just wanted to reserve a table for us. I waved to you."

But then, Paula realized there was something else going on, something deeper. Her experience told her to ask Andrea about her feelings: "Why did you feel abandoned?" And, even though she thought there was no reason for Andrea to feel that way, she acknowledged and honored those feelings. She realized that Andrea needed to hear that it was not her intention to abandon her, and moreover that she really was concerned about her when Andrea did not come back. Paula hoped that her willingness to listen to Andrea now would serve as further proof of her concern.

Paula began by telling Andrea about the many times she left the dinner to try to call her. "I was really worried about you," she reassured her. "I didn't know what happened. I thought maybe you got sick. I looked for you until they told me you weren't coming back, and then I called four times."

Then, as Andrea began to reveal how upset and sad she was, Paula listened. Even though Paula thought Andrea was wrong to leave like that without telling her, she didn't try to contradict her. She tried instead to understand, because now she realized the extent of Andrea's pain. She also realized that what Andrea needed most at that moment was reassurance, support, and some evidence of her care and concern.

Apparently, Andrea's upset had started with the rain and the umbrella. Andrea had suddenly felt very alienated from Paula, as Paula walked ahead quickly. Paula's pace seemed so fast to her, since she had just come from a slow-moving rural environment. Yet, she felt unable to say anything, not knowing how to put her feelings of alienation into words. At the desk in the church these feelings intensified, when there was some confusion about the reservations Paula had made and the arrangements for both to pay separately. Next, when Paula bounded ahead into the room, Andrea felt left behind once again. And when she looked into the room that looked like a soup kitchen and saw Paula far ahead looking for a table, the feeling of being cast aside swept over her like an evil mist.

"I just had to leave," Andrea explained. "I just needed to be back in the safety of the place I was staying. Everything seemed so alienating and degrading. I felt like I had been giving so much to help others with my work, and I suddenly felt so unappreciated. It was like I was alone in this place that looked like a cafeteria for the Salvation Army, and I thought to myself: 'Am

I reduced to this?' I felt so hopeless and worthless. I needed to escape; to be by myself."

It's lucky for both of them that Paula had the experience to pick up on Andrea's cues about her feelings of being abandoned and worthless. Paula responded appropriately by validating and reassuring her. The situation might easily had become even more painful and hostile for each of them, had Paula fired back with her own resentment. Instead, even though Paula felt like she had done nothing wrong, she tried to see her own behavior from Andrea's point of view. She said how sorry she was that Andrea had gotten the wrong impression from what she did at the church, and pointed out that she most certainly was concerned about Andrea. Then, to further demonstrate her concern and to make Andrea feel more important, she encouraged Andrea to talk out her feelings. Paula listened, with occasional comments to show Andrea that she understood how she could feel as she did. Andrea was reluctant to talk at first. She saw Paula as one more person who had let her down over the few days she had been back in San Francisco. But Paula managed to push the right buttons by being sensitive to what Andrea needed at the time. Andrea really did feel listened to, understood, and important.

The incident with Paula had triggered the response it did, because it occurred at a time when Andrea was already experiencing a great deal of loneliness, alienation, and sadness. Andrea was especially sensitive, and ready to interpret what Paula did as just another betrayal of trust and friendship. But Paula was able to overcome the conflict and break through the barrier of misunderstandings created by Andrea's special needs at this time by being aware, ready to listen and respond, and willing to see things from Andrea's point of view, rather than her own. In the end, their friendship was restored, even deepened. Once the problem was resolved, they made plans to meet again and talk about the possibility of a future collaboration. After that meeting went well, they made further arrangements for the future. "And it's all because I was able to pick up what Andrea really needed when I called her to find out what happened," said Paula. "Otherwise, I would have probably just returned the clothes she had left in my care to a friend of hers, and that would have been the end. I'm sure we would hever have worked together again."

Should you be in a situation where someone becomes very emotional or appears to overact, this is generally an indicator that something about the situation has tapped into some deep inner needs and you need to address these to resolve the problem and repair the relationship. In particular, you might keep in mind these steps:

- If the person's reaction seems very intense and out of proportion to the kind of response expected in that situation, stop and think to yourself: What kind of deeper problems or needs might this reflect?
- Try to put yourself in the other person's shoes and imagine how things might look to this other person: what might this person be thinking about the situation?
- Consider your own behavior in light of the other person's point of view. Is there anything you might have done that could be misinterpreted?
- Consider whether the other person might be under special pressures right now that might have triggered the response.
- Think about what you might say to gently open up the possibility of talking about the real issues.
- Show that you are sensitive and really do care about the other person and his or her point of view; indicate that you are willing to take the time to be patient and really understand.
- Be willing to put your own needs aside in order to put a priority on listening to the other person's concerns. Later you can express your own needs; but right now it is important to show the other person you value him or her and want to satisfy his or her needs, because he or she seems to be in very much pain.

Meeting Mutual Needs

In the above case, the conflict was resolved because one person in the conflict put her own needs on hold to focus on the more serious needs of the other. But there can be many times in conflict situations where your own needs are equally important, although you'll still have to meet the other person's needs to solve the problem. In this case, a key to resolution is finding some approach that can satisfy both of you. This usually means you'll have to get down to the real needs underlying the apparent cause of the conflict.

A situation like this took place between Julie and her landlord, Tayna. Tayna lived upstairs in the townhouse the two women shared. Julie had been living there for about two years, and had every intention of staying. She was in a Ph.D. graduate program at a nearby school, and the apartment was ideal for her needs. She also felt she had developed a good, friendly relationship with her landlord. About a year earlier, their original one-year lease had expired, and she had stayed on a month-by-month basis. The arrangement seemed fine for everyone, or so she thought.

The problem started when Tayna said she wanted to draw up a lease, just to protect herself in case Julie moved out suddenly, without sufficient notice. "No problem," said Julie. She thought Tayna just wanted to reformalize their existing arrangement. Since Julie had no intention of leaving, she was perfectly satisfied to sign a lease for a year or two, based on the arrangement they already had.

But when Tayna came down to see her one morning, Julie found it *wasn't* the same arrangement that had been working well for so long. Tayna had added a number of changes. One was a whopping 14 percent increase in the rent. Tayna explained that the place was a real bargain, since it would rent for much more on the open market. Besides, she said, Julie was there most of the day, since she studied and worked out of the apartment, rather than going out to work like most tenants. And then there were several new provisions. For one thing, Tayna wanted an extra $1500 security deposit. She was concerned that when Julie gave notice, she might not be able to show the place immediately because Julie had so many books and shelves in the place. Tayna also required a written request from Julie to have any business groups over for the workshops Julie often led. Tayna assured her: "Of course, I'll normally say yes. I just want to know what's going on." Even so, Julie was incensed that Tayna demanded a written notice about an activity she had been carrying on for two years without any problem. Finally, there was a penalty clause stating that if the rent wasn't paid by the 5th of the month, there would be a $100 penalty, plus 8 percent monthly interest. If a check bounced, Tayna wanted $20 for check costs.

Julie tried to express some of her concerns, particularly about all the extra money she would have to come up with. But Tayna just brushed these off. "Oh, we're not affected by the city's policies on rent control here, because it's an owner occupied building. We can set any rent we want. . . And besides, you'll get back your extra security deposit when you move out, assuming no damage. You'll even get interest on the money." When Julie explained that she would have to pay much more interest than she would ever get back, because she would have to borrow at exorbitant rates from her credit cards, Tayna again just shrugged off her concerns. "Oh, well, that's not my problem."

Then, standing up, Tayna announced, "Well, I'll just leave the contract for you to look over," and left.

When Julie reviewed the contract, she was even more upset. The more she thought about it, the more she found the contract and her whole exchange with Tayna disturbing. Both were overly impersonal, meanspirited, and implied suspicion about everything she did. Moreover, she had been living as Tayna's tenant for over two years without any problems; shouldn't that count for something? Tayna seemed to treat her like she could be anyone walking in off the street.

The next day, Julie wrote Tayna a letter expressing her feelings. She allowed that she could "probably manage the rent increase," although she pointed out that it was much higher than the usual annual rent increases. She described her reasons for not feeling comfortable with the other lease provisions. And she concluded by stating that although she had been planning to stay for at least another two years, her discomfort with the lease provisions made her wonder whether she should stay at all. "Accordingly, I would like a few more days to think through what I would like to do," she wrote, "and I will of course give you 30 days' notice." Two days later, while Tayna was out of town and hadn't even gotten her first note, Julie made her decision to move and put her 30-day notice note under Tayna's door.

Julie's decision was exactly what Tayna *didn't* want. What she did want was a firmer commitment from Julie to stay there. She also wanted to be sure that if Julie did move she wouldn't do so suddenly or without cleaning up the place. Otherwise, Tayna was afraid it would be difficult to show the place so she could arrange to have a new tenant to replace Julie as soon as she moved out. But of course, none of that came through in their discussion. Rather, Julie felt like she was being viewed as a stranger coming in off the street to rent an apartment, and that Tayna's only concern was the dollar sign. No wonder Julie wanted to move. She felt humiliated and demeaned, not even considering the extra financial burden.

When Tanya returned from her weekend trip to find Julie's letter, she saw none of this. Just as Tanya's real needs were unclear to Julie, Julie's real needs were concealed from Tanya. All Tanya could see was that Julie was moving, and when she called her up, she was very angry. "Your moving so suddenly is just what I was afraid of. That's why I needed the lease," she said angrily. "I think you're taking advantage of me. And you'll be moving right before Christmas, which is the worst possible time for me to rent the place."

"But you're the one who suddenly changed the terms of the lease," Julie protested. "That's the reason I'm moving; not because I originally wanted to."

Each was upset, and blamed the other for the outcome neither wanted—Julie moving. They practically hung up on each other. Each still thought it was a dispute about money and legal terms in a lease. In fact, it was about much more: both parties' unexpressed needs.

The situation might have ended on this sad note, with Julie moving at this worst possible time for them both. But then, because she was so busy now, Julie wrote a note asking for a few extra days, or even weeks, so she could get her things organized. That way, too, she would be under less immediate pressure to find a new place. She pointed out that it would give Tanya more time to show the place, and she would have the time to clean it up so Tanya could show it more effectively. As a final thought, she added: "Perhaps we might also talk about some of my reactions to the lease you left me, so you don't feel I'm trying to take advantage of you. I actually felt you were trying to do this to me. Apart from any financial considerations, the provisions in the new lease made me uncomfortable about staying here for various reasons."

The letter turned out to be just what was needed. It opened the door to exploring the real needs of both Julie and Tanya, so both could end up getting what they really wanted. After she saw the letter, Tanya called Julie to set up a meeting, and Julie agreed. Then, at the meeting in Julie's apartment, Tanya began by saying: "Okay, let's backtrack to the way things were before I gave you the new lease." Tanya explained her concerns and fears that led her to write up such a strict lease.

Everything was going wrong in my life at the time. A close relative had died. I had some unexpected difficulties at work. And then I had problems with other relatives about some family matters. I felt like I needed more stability and security in my life, and that's when I wrote up the lease. I wasn't really thinking about how you might feel about it, and I really do feel you are a good tenant, and want you to stay. The lease wasn't meant as an ultimatum, just something for you to look at so we could talk about it. Maybe we can still work things out, if you'd consider staying.

The result of Tanya's revelations about her own problems and her appreciation for Julie worked like magic. Within about ten minutes, the two women had worked out an agreement. It turned out to be surprisingly easy, since their real desires and needs were actually complementary. First, it became clear that neither wanted the move. The question was one of eliminating the difficulties that led to the threat. There was the extra security deposit Tanya had asked for, for starters. The only reason she wanted it was her fear of not being able to show the apartment if Julie left the apartment messy after giving notice, or didn't give enough notice. When Julie agreed to make sure the apartment was in reasonable shape for showing, and to give an extra week of notice, the issue was resolved. With this major hurdle overcome, the other objectionable provisions fell one by one. Since Tanya realized how much she valued Julie as a tenant, after almost losing her, she dropped the rent increase. Also, realizing that Julie had given her no problems with guests or rent payments for two years, Tanya dropped the new permission and penalty clauses. She assured Julie these had been triggered by unrelated, personal fears.

Julie finally agreed to stay and sign the lease. Perhaps as important as the financial concessions Tanya made were the assurances she gave Julie that she was a valued person and tenant. It was a reassurance Julie needed—that Tanya really liked her and wanted her there.

By opening themselves up, by sharing what they really needed and wanted, both Julie and Tanya were able to satisfy their needs. In fact, as a result of the near disaster, both came to appreciate each other more. After that, their relationship became noticeably warmer. They still related as landlord and tenant, and not as personal or social friends. But they greeted each other more warmly in the halls or on the street. They called on each more and more often for neighborly sorts of things— such as accepting packages for one another. And Julie also found that suddenly Tanya was much more responsive when she called about replacing burned out lightbulbs or turning up the heat. It was as if they were both relieved that Julie was staying, that they both wanted to make sure now that the relationship continued to work.

This process of discovering needs may sound a little like a mystery game to you. But then, part of resolving conflicts is the process of discovering what is causing the conflict. And while you'll have to rely on some intuition, there are steps you can take to make the process less of a guessing game and more of a sure way to get to the heart of the problem. After all, recognizing the true problem is halfway towards solving it.

Often, a conflict may appear to be a win-lose situation—i.e., the tenant pays more or less rent, and the landlord gets more or less money. But the true problems or issues may lie beneath the surface. Each person may have other more important needs that he or she wants to satisfy (such as long-term stability; feeling needed and valued as a person; having a responsible tenant who regularly pays the rent and shows consideration and concern for the place). If these needs can be uncovered, it suddenly becomes possible to satisfy both parties. Thus, a key to resolving conflict is finding an opening to bring up those needs (such as writing a letter to invite discussion) and getting away from the original positions where both persons are stuck to find alternative solutions.

The next section includes a case history that will illustrate this process for you. But the following points are good to keep in mind. They are general guidelines for getting unstuck by responding to mutual needs.

- If you feel someone's initial position is impossible for you, but there might still be something in it for you if you can soften that position, don't take that position as an ultimatum.
- Open up the door to further discussion if you can, say by writing a letter or making a phone call to talk about the situation and perhaps find some mutually satisfying resolution.
- Find out why the person has taken the position he or she has; in other words, look for the person's real needs underneath.
- Think about your own underlying needs; ask what is really most important to you.
- Consider some possibilities that might satisfy both of your needs, or think about ways of giving up some things that are less important to you and more important to the other person in return for things that are more important to you and less so for the other.
- Share your concerns calmly and listen respectfully. Emphasize your desire to solve the problem and focus on solutions, not recriminations and anger over what has happened before.

Discovering Hidden Needs and Fears

In the previous examples, it was possible to resolve a conflict by getting needs and fears out in the open so they could be discussed and resolved. Once everybody's true concerns were addressed, the conflict melted away. In fact, the people in these examples actually developed warmer relationships as a result of the conflict: it triggered a revelation of needs that led to greater openness and shared understandings.

In some cases, however, this revelation may be especially hard to achieve. People in conflict often conceal their real needs and fears, or even fail to recognize them. The conflicts in their lives continue until these real needs are discovered and addressed. And so it becomes necessary to dig to discover what's going on—in the other person, in yourself, or in both of you. You might choose to let the other person hold on to a fiction if he or she doesn't want to admit his real needs or fears. But if you sense that these underlying needs or fears are really motivating the person, you must respond to these underlying sources of motivation—not to the apparent needs or fears that are expressed.

For example, this process of discovery is what helped Arlene achieve a satisfactory ghost-writing arrangement with another woman. The other woman had repeatedly changed her mind about exactly what type of writing arrangement she wanted: a co-authorship in which she paid less and gave up half of the royalties; a ghostwriting-but-shared-royalty arrangement in which she paid somewhat more in return for the writer taking a smaller but substantial percentage of the royalties; or a straight ghost-writing arrangement, which strained her budget.

The arrangement started successfully enough after Mary Beth hired Arlene to ghostwrite a proposal on relationships, with Mary Beth supplying the notes and transcripts for counseling sessions. Arlene's job was simply to turn them into a proposal, and then to help Mary Beth find a publisher for them. The conflict started after Arlene did find a publisher, but the advance was only $3000, not enough to fully cover Arlene's ghostwriter fee. Still, the chance of finding another publisher with a higher advance was iffy.

So Arlene came up with what she thought was the ideal solution to enable Mary Beth to publish her book, gain the credibility and recognition it would bring, yet not bust her budget. Instead of ghostwriting the book on a straight fee basis, Arlene offered to work for half of her usual fee in return for half of the royalties and her name on the book as the writer "with" Mary Beth.

In a brief letter, Arlene outlined her proposal. She viewed it strictly as a business proposition, one she thought especially fair since it offered Mary Beth the option to either choose the arrangement, or to change her mind at any time before the book contract was signed, and instead simply pay Arlene her regular fee as a ghostwriter.

But when Mary Beth called to respond to the proposal, she was livid. She didn't think Arlene was being fair at all—she complained she was asking too much, since she would end up with over half the book (half the royalties plus her agent's commission). On top of this, Arlene would be getting credit. Meanwhile, Mary Beth protested; she was spending a great deal of time and energy on the book herself, plus incurring expenses for transcripts and typing.

In response, Arlene tried to offer some alternatives, such as deducting the expenses before the split or dropping her request for credit in return for the first income from the book paid to her. But the problem was that the two women understood the issue differently. To Arlene, it was simply the negotiation of a business deal, in which her main interest was to get paid for her work, while the credit was at least something she could show for the risk she had taken if she didn't get any additional money. But to Mary Beth, the book was much more; she had a huge emotional investment in it.

Since they were coming from such very different places, and Arlene initially was unaware of Mary Beth's concerns, she found it very difficult to talk to Mary Beth. Each time she offered another suggestion about how the two might work together, she felt like she was walking on eggs. Almost anything, it seemed, might set Mary Beth off. One time, after Arlene had suggested another fee agreement (Arlene would be paid more up front in return for a reduced royalty, so Mary Beth retained more of the book), Mary Beth raised the issue of trust. She had never before questioned Arlene's integrity, but now she wondered aloud if Arlene would bill her for the correct number of hours she spent on the project. How could she know? How could she be sure? Mary Beth even speculated that maybe she should hire another writer.

The discussions went on and on, with each woman increasingly offended. Mary Beth continued to waver about what to do: pay Arlene more for less royalty and credit, or pay Arlene less and give up more royalty and control. And then there was her concern about money. What did she really want? And what could she afford to do? Meanwhile, Arlene was finalizing the contract with the publisher, and something had to be settled between them about the authorship and royalty agreement if the book was going to proceed at all.

Finally, feeling a sense of desperation and exhaustion about the whole process, which had dragged on for about two months, Arlene sent Mary Beth one last letter. In it, she listed the various options. The list of options included those the women had already discussed, plus one last suggestion Arlene threw in as an afterthought to respond to Mary Beth's concern about the money. If Arlene could be listed as a co-author and share the royalties equally, Mary Beth wouldn't have to pay her anything more, beyond covering any additional out-of-pocket expenses. It was actually Arlene's least desired alternative, because in return for the extra credit, it meant getting no money at all if the book didn't do well. And potentially this could mean many more hours on the project, since now Mary Beth would be paying her nothing. But in her frustration just to see some agreement to get the book published, she threw this out as a possibility. She really didn't think Mary Beth would go for this either, since it meant sharing the credit as well as the royalties on Mary Beth's only book.

But to her surprise, a few days later, when Mary Beth called, that was the proposal she decided to choose. And now it was too late to back down. So Arlene agreed, and when the contract arrived, she filled in the sections based on their agreement. The process seemed routine, and so, without thinking much about it, Arlene divided up the number of books going to the author equally between herself and Mary Beth. After all, she thought, that would be the logical thing to do if they were now co-authors.

But then, when she sent the contract to Mary Beth for her final approval and signature, that single clause proved the sticking point. It suddenly brough home to Mary Beth the real problem with the agreement: she didn't want to share the co-authorship, and when she gave up her sole control to Arlene, she·didn't really think through what it meant. At the time, none of this was clear to either Mary Beth or Arlene. But it was clear that this clause tapped something deep within Mary Beth, because once again, she suddenly exploded, coming up with all sorts of reasons about why she felt uncomfortable about work-ing with Arlene and why she didn't trust her. For example, she complained, why was Arlene suddenly asking for half of these books now, when it was Mary Beth's idea to ask the publisher for 25 books instead of 10? And if Arlene could do this, how could she trust her as a co-author? Would she have to keep her eye out for every little thing? Then, when Arlene tried to explain her reasons and offered to give up the extra books, Mary Beth wasn't willing to listen. She was still upset and talking about trust and betrayal.

This time, it really looked like things were going to fall apart for good. But then, Arlene sensed what was really going on for Mary Beth. Outwardly, Mary Beth indicated that she was con-cerned about the money, and acted to keep down the amount of money she spent. Thus, she agreed to the co-authorship arrangement. But in reality, what she wanted was the credit. She wanted to maintain the control and ownership of the book; and her inner self was fighting against giving this up, while her outer self was seeking to do this to save money. Thus, when she saw the changed contract term about the books, it was really an excuse—a way to get herself out of an agreement she really didn't want, although externally she spoke as if this is what she wanted.

The insight came to Arlene in a flash. Perhaps it was Mary Beth's intense anger over something seemingly so trivial. Perhaps it was this awareness combined with all the back and forth discussions. Whatever the reason, acting purely on instinct, Arlene did what was probably the one thing she could to save her relationship with Mary Beth and the book. She spoke to what were Mary Beth's real needs and fears, not to what Mary Beth had been saying they were.

"Look, I really don't need my name on any more books," Arlene said. "I'm not trying to take this book away from you. I've just asked for the percentage and the credits on the book because of the extra risk I'm taking in not getting paid. That's all. I don't want the credit. This is your book."

And with that, the tension that had been building suddenly vanished. It was as if Arlene's statement was right on target, and suddenly Mary Beth too realized what she really wanted—the credit, ownership, and control of this book. The money issue was important, but secondarily. She wanted this to fully be her own book.

The result was that Arlene and Mary Beth finally did work out an agreement. Arlene became a ghostwriter again, just as they had arranged in the beginning. But this time, to take care of Mary Beth's insecurities about whether the book would actually be accepted, Arlene agreed to receive only half of the payment when she completed the manuscript. Then, she would get the rest on acceptance.

And so the book did go forward, for the conflict was resolved. As Arlene recognized, Mary Beth's inner needs and fears were in effect at war with her apparent external concerns. So that inner conflict needed to be resolved first, to resolve the external conflict. As a result, by helping Mary Beth recognize her real needs and fears and resolve that inner conflict, Arlene helped to resolve the external one over whether Arlene should ghostwrite or co-author the book. Initially, Mary Beth's concerns over money blocked the ghostwriting possibility. But then, as it became clear that the publication, credit, and control of the book were really what mattered to Mary Beth, it became clear that the book needed to be hers alone. The ghostwriting arrangement was the only way to go. These real needs had been obscure to both Arlene and Mary Beth in the beginning. They were hard to discover under Mary Beth's emotional turmoil, and because her actions and words concealed her real motivations. But eventually, hints of this reality peeked through, and clearly it was necessary to discover and acknowledge these real concerns to resolve the conflict.

Similarly, if you are in a situation where someone is very emotional about something, seems ambivalent and uncertain about what he or she wants, and you are having a difficult time in achieving a resolution that might be beneficial to both of you, take the time to look underneath the surface for hidden needs or fears. Some ways to do this include the following steps:

- Look for clues that suggest what the person may really want, but hasn't admitted to you or to himself. Notice what the person is resisting or what the person gets upset about as a clue to what the person really doesn't want, even though he may claim that is what he wants. (For example, in the case just described, Mary Beth was resisting entering into a co-authorship agreement, although outwardly she said this is what she wanted, and the key point in the contract that made her so upset was the sharing of the books, which would be a natural outcome of a co-authority agreement based on equally sharing the fruits of the book.)
- Come up with a suggested proposal that you think might meet those hidden needs. If the person feels it does meet these needs, the proposal might break a log jam. If not, the person can always turn the proposal down. (For example, this is what Arlene did in saying that she didn't really want any credit for the book and was just asking for the credit because of the extra risk she was taking in not getting paid. But she emphasized that it was Mary Beth's book—exactly what Mary Beth really wanted; so the log jam was broken. Mary Beth could acknowledge that the credit came first for her, the money was secondary; so now she was willing to come up with the money to achieve what she really wanted—and what Arlene really wanted too).

- Be willing to put your own needs on the table, because you want to get your own needs satisfied too, as well as satisfying the other person. Once these true needs are out in the open, you are both in a better position to come up with alternatives that will be satisfying to you both. (For example, this is what Arlene did when she emphasized that her first interest was in making money; and credit was secondary to her. In turn, once both sets of needs were on the table, it was obvious they were compatible—for Mary Beth, the credit and control came first; the money was secondary; for Arlene, the money came first, and she really didn't care about credit and control. So now they could both work together and get what they really wanted; not the co-authorship arrangement that was what each one wanted least).

Putting the Other's Needs First

It's an accomplishment to recognize another person's true needs—and be able to act on them. This is especially true if those needs don't correspond perfectly with your own (as will often be the case, unfortunately). Ideally, you'll each grant something, and gain something. But the toughest challenge of all can be those cases that require you to recognize the *priority* of someone else's needs over your own. Sometimes, this recognition can be the only effective way of resolving the conflict. The other person just might be needier at the moment of the conflict, or more emotionally upset about it. Or perhaps that person simply has more power than you in the conflict situation. These are all compelling reasons to satisfy the other person's needs or fears first, in order to move to the next step of working out a rational resolution to the problem. This does *not* mean giving up on your own needs. It just means you may need to put them off for a while, must get them met in a more round-about or circumspect way from this person, or maybe you need to get these needs met somewhere else.

Sally, a woman who felt like she was hopelessly tangled in a bureaucratic snarl, realized that she was in just such a situation. Part of the problem, she said, was that the official in charge of making decisions didn't like her and was trying to make things difficult for her. The whole thing began when Sally was ready to begin an extern position in her psychology program. The placement director, Mr. W., had listened in detail to the kind of work experience she wanted. He then suggested a work program in which Sally would work part-time in a half-way house for substance abusers. It sounded ideal to her. She felt she could have some hands-on experience for the first time in a field that fascinated her.

But after Sally started, she found the job was not at all what she expected. Instead of spending her time helping in therapy sessions or getting to talk one-on-one with the patients, she found herself assigned to do many center chores. "I was doing things like helping to prepare meals and doing gardening in the yard. I didn't feel like I was doing what I was trained for," she said.

So Sally went to speak to Mr. W. about being placed in another program. At first, he tried to convince her to work things out where she was. Maybe she could talk to the director at the center? But no, Sally said she had already tried that. Mr. W. pointed out how hard it was to find new placements in the middle of the term. Maybe it wouldn't be possible to find her a new program; could she at least stick it out? No, no, she couldn't, she argued, because she felt insulted and demeaned in her role. She also claimed there were hard feelings between herself and some of the center's staff members since she had tried to get them to make changes so her work would be more suitable. The discussion with Mr. W. went on and on, almost rising to the level of a heated argument at points. Finally, Mr. W. agreed. He would terminate her from the place where she was, and try to find her something else. Still, Sally could see he was annoyed by her determination to leave. Sally waited a few weeks, while Mr. W. presumably called around. Since nothing turned up immediately, she also began to make a few calls herself. And then she found what seemed like the perfect solution—another drug program with outpatients, where she could assist with both intake interviews and facilitating group sessions. Plus she could help in the recreational program.

She made an appointment to see Mr. W. about making placement arrangements. When she met with him, though, he announced with enthusiasm that he had found another program for her after extensive efforts. In fact, to speed up the process of change, he had enrolled her in the progrm and completed all the paperwork. Now all she had to do was sign the necessary agreements, and she could begin.

Sally, of course, had already found another program. Perhaps at this point, some kind of agreement might have been worked out—had Sally and Mr. W. been able to talk reasonably about the two options. Mr. W. might even have been persuaded to let Sally participate in the program she had found. But as soon as he spoke of his own efforts to find something suitable, Sally became very upset. She spoke with growing intensity of her need to find a proper placement: of her desire to have the kind of responsibility and training offered by the place she had found; of her uncertainties about the place Mr. W. had found. She also implied that the school had been lax in not finding her the proper placement in the first place (and that it was slow in finding her a new one). Meanwhile, as the intensity level of the discussion rose, Mr. W. accused her of being very inflexible. He said that perhaps he should terminate her not only from the new placement, but from the entire program as well. Sally finally stormed out of his office in a rage.

It was at this point that she came to me for advice on what to do. The offer to get into the program Mr. W. had come up with was still available; but she really wanted to get into the program she had found. It seemed like Mr. W. was blocking the way. He wanted her to go into the program he had found for her and wouldn't even consider her suggestion—because, she said, he didn't like her.

"I think he just resents my independence and determination," Sally told me. "I don't think he's used to having students take initiative or think for themselves. He'd just like to see everyone fit in and be docile."

Sally wondered if the thing to do now was to appeal over the placement director's head. "I could bring the whole thing before the school's field committee, or threaten to," she suggested. "Then maybe he'd back down. I don't think it's fair to kick me out of the program just because I don't want to accept a placement that might not be appropriate for me."

As Sally went on, she made it clear that she was gearing up for an all-out battle with the placement director and her school. It sounded like she was ready to call on the National Guard or the ACLU, to help her assert her rights against a placement director who insulted her, was prejudiced against her, and was on the verge of terminating her from the school's placement program just because she had dared to be independent.

Many of her points were valid. But was this confrontation really the best strategy to get what she wanted? If Mr. W. already thought she was inflexible, this strategy might convince him even more. And if he was threatened by her independence and initiative, wouldn't her actions pose even more of a threat? Besides, he *had* tried to find her another placement that was more suitable than the first. Shouldn't he be recognized and validated for that? Then, too, regardless of Sally's personal feelings, Mr. W. had the advantage of power in the situation. He was in the position to approve or deny her access to the school placement program. It was in her best interest to be on his good side, if possible, and avoid a direct confrontation, because if the situation escalated into an official challenge to his power, most probably Mr. W. would win.

The more we discussed the matter, the more it became clear that the best strategy for getting what she really wanted—if possible, the placement she had found, and at the very least remaining in the program—was to look at the issue from Mr. W.'s point of view. What might address *his* needs? Sure, Sally had her own needs—to be independent, to be self-fulfilled in her work. But these needs were probably best met by taking care of Mr. W's needs first. He would then be in a position to help *her*.

One key need of Mr. W.'s, it seemed, was to feel in control. As Sally described her various confrontations with him at more length, it seemed that what really triggered his anger was the way in which her efforts to take the initiative, combined with her spirit of determination, challenged his authority. What she probably needed to do was just the opposite of what she first proposed. Instead of coming on strong and threatening the exercise of her legal rights, which might only escalate the confrontation, she should probably approach him contritely and apologetically. She should appear conciliatory, and indicate that she was very sorry if she seemed to challenge him. Also, she might acknowledge his efforts on her behalf to secure her a better placement. The approach seemed less distasteful when Sally recognized the truth in it—from Mr. W.'s perspective. She also saw that this approach did not involve conceding anything she wanted. In fact, it reopened the door of opportunity. Then, after she had cooled things down and led Mr. W. to understand that his own efforts had been recognized and appreciated, she might gently explain her side. What had gotten her so upset, she might say truthfully, was that she had found a program she really liked and felt was very appropriate. If Mr. W. thought it possible, that's the one she wanted to do. Besides, she might point out that this program would contribute to her learning at the school, and wasn't that one of his objectives for his students?

Since the key issue from Mr. W.'s point of view was a student challenging an administrator's authority, her strategy should be to acknowledge and accept his authority and show her contrition in trying to challenge him so stridently. Thus, though she might feel it somewhat humbling or even humiliating to do so, her best approach was, as I told her,

> to throw yourself at this man's mercy; acknowledge his power; reinforce his authority; show your appreciation; seek his forgiveness. You might feel angry and hurt yourself, but ultimately you're addressing your own needs. Focus on how *he* must feel, realizing that you are likely to get more by seeing the struggle from his point of view. The person in power is, after all, usually the person who has the most power to decide the outcome of the situation.

The upshot of this discussion was that Sally did decide to try this strategy. She wrote Mr. W. a very gentle, apologetic letter to smooth the way. When she met with him, she presented herself and her case as we had described. And it worked like magic, she reported back. At once, Mr. W. softened. He said that perhaps he had been too harsh in threatening to terminate her from the program. He admitted that he should be more appreciative of her initiative in trying to find a better program for her. Accordingly, he agreed to meet with the director of the program she had located. He would discuss the arrangements with the director, and if it met with the school standards, he would be pleased to have her enter the program. In fact, he suggested at the end of the meeting, that if the program was up to standards then perhaps he could include it in the range of programs offered to other students who sought placements, and if so, he would have to thank Sally for that.

About a week later, Sally learned that Mr. W. had met with the director and approved her placement in the program she wanted. By giving Mr. W. what he wanted or needed in that particular confrontation, Sally ended up getting her own way. It had been hard at first for her to mask her own independence and desire for power to give in, but meeting the other party's needs for control and authority required this. The resolution hinged on meeting *his* needs, since he was the one in power; but also on *her* ability to read his needs, address them, and do so in such a way as to meet her own ultimate ends. Sally's situation might have ended up worse than it already was had the conflict continued to escalate. Then she surely wouldn't have gotten what she wanted and might have even ended up with nothing. Instead, there was a win-win resolution for them both. They both got their needs met—and the process began by Sally first meeting Mr. W.'s needs.

If you are in a situation where it appears necessary to satisfy the other person's needs to resolve the conflict, and the other person is in a position of power so you can't just walk away from the problem or force through your own agenda, some keys to achieving a satisfying resolution for yourself are the following:

- Notice what the other person's needs are if these are apparent from what the person is saying or doing (i.e., being in control of the situation; achieving your acquiescence to his power; etc.)
- If you aren't clear what the other person's needs are, ask questions to find out what the other person wants and

listen carefully to what he or she says; sometimes the person may be clear in stating personal needs; other times these needs may be buried between the lines, and you may need to use your intuition to find them. (Some questions to a person in a power position might be things like· "What would you like me to do?" "How can I help you achieve _____?" "Is there something I did that is bothering you?")

- If you feel that a key issue for this person is the question of control or a fear of being challenged—and that person really is in a position of power relative to you—be humble, apologetic, and self- effacing if necessary, to help that person to feel more secure, powerful, and unchallenged. Being tough in such a situation will only tend to make that person be defensive and respond by showing how he or she can exert power over you, which will very likely mean not giving you what you want. Once the other person feels secure in his power, then you can calmly, rationally, and gently ask for what you really want in a way that shows deference to the other person. In turn, by massaging the other person's feelings, he or she will be more likely to accede to your request. After all, if he or she can now give you what you want from a position of power, that is a way of affirming his or her own power. In short, by giving up your own power, you can help yourself get what you want in such a situation; whereas to show off your power may be just the action which will prevent achieving your goal. You'll probably just escalate the conflict, but not get what you want.

Summing Up

In sum, one key to resolving a conflict is looking for the under-lying needs you and the other party have. Addressing these can enable you to work out a resolution. As the foregoing examples illustrate, there are four key considerations when you do this:

- Just *recognizing another person's needs and fears*—and then talking about them and responding to them—can some-times be enough to resolve the conflict.

- Recognizing the other's needs and *sharing your own needs* can allow you to work out an arrangement that satisfies you both.
- At times, you may have to *look for hidden needs and fears that underlie stated ones,* in order to respond to the real needs and fears that are producing the conflict.
- And sometimes, you may have to *place a priority on resolving the other party's needs first* in order to satisfy your own.

6

Overcoming Conflicts Through Better Communication

Communication, the key to resolving most conflicts, is itself often the *cause* of conflict. Any breakdown of communication can lead to conflict; and there are numerous examples in everyday interactions. Sometimes one person isn't clear. Sometimes someone isn't listening. There are often misunderstandings about meanings. Hidden assumptions can stand in the way. And sometimes there is no communication at all, resulting in misunderstandings, hostility, or resentment. Happily, you can harness the tremendous power of communication to break these blocks. A little knowledge and practice will help you send out an appropriate message which is accurately heard and returned.

The key is to keep in mind the basic principles of communication. Many of the principles may sound like common sense. Even so, people commonly remain unaware of them, and that makes miscommunication—and thus conflict—more likely. In addition, once the emotions become triggered in a conflict, it won't always be easy to draw consciously on these principles. But if you develop a constant awareness of them, you'll be able to avert potential conflicts before they begin or reach full pitch. You'll even be able to respond effectively—and almost instinctively—if you do find yourself mid-battle.

This chapter highlights these basic principles. You might try reading through them all at once, and then focusing on one at a time. Can you think of similar examples from your life? Spend a day or two paying close attention to people communicating around you. Chances are you'll find ample examples of each typical error. You might then think of ways to correct the error (but it's usually best to keep your awareness to yourself, since others may not appreciate your corrections of them). The principles and remedies outlined below should help you make these corrections.

The Discrepancy Between Non-Verbal and Verbal Communication

Experts in the communication field tell us that we get about 55 percent of our information from the *non-verbal* communication that accompanies a spoken message (such as facial gestures and body movements). We get about 38 percent from the voice, pitch, tone, and sounds we hear; and only 7 percent from content. This means that we're remarkably likely to misinterpret or discredit the very message someone thinks he or she is communicating. We might hear one thing, but if we sense that someone really feels or means something else (from that person's non-verbal or voice cues), trust can break down or we may react to that person negatively or inappropriately. If someone seems nervous, for instance, no matter how cogent the message, we may not believe or fully credit it. If someone apologizes, but seems hesitant and therefore insincere, we may feel even angrier.

Accordingly, if you are speaking and feel a sense of distrust, distance, or negativity growing between you and the other person, stop for a minute. Ask yourself if that could be due to this kind of discrepancy between the message you want to convey and the way you are presenting it. Body language is often unwilled—but it can be controlled. With this awareness, you can try to bring things back into alignment. For example, act humble if you're apologizing. Look your listener in the eye if your message is an important one (eye contact is perceived as a sign of sincerity). You might actually mention the lack of alignment you perceive to reassure the other person.

To illustrate, picture a husband and wife having a quarrel. Part of the problem is that the wife doesn't believe the husband when he says he loves her. He has trouble showing his feelings. So the words come across as just that—words. Meanwhile, the wife is imagining the worst—another woman. The husband might be able to help short-circuit the conflict by admitting his difficulty in expressing his feelings. He might even admit that he understands her lack of trust in him; it's his own failure to convey his sincerity adequately. With this revelation, the wife might better understand the real reason for her mistrust. The conversation becomes more anchored in reality, and this helps to defuse conflict.

Conversely, if you experience this discrepancy between verbal and non-verbal content in someone else, it might help to bring that out in the open. For example, such a discrepancy might consist of the following out-of-phase words, gestures, tones, or body movements.

- a smile indicating friendliness, but a cold, hostile tone of voice, clenched hands, or a movement away from you indicating anger or dislike
- a message proclaiming trust and a close, warm relationship, but a hesitant manner and shifting eye-contact, suggesting a lack of confidence or sincerity
- an aggressive tone and words of attack, suggesting anger and blame directed towards you, combined with a tentative, halting manner and shaking hands, suggesting the person is really not confident or sure of himself

You probably already have your own directory of what these non-verbal body cues mean to you, and a careful study of body language will make you even more aware.

Then, by calling attention to the discrepancy you notice, you can show the person you aren't convinced by what he or she is saying or are confused by the difference between what he or she is saying and doing, and want to understand what the person really means. Make these points in a non-hostile, non-threatening way if you can, using a gentle, tentative tone of voice to say something about what you perceive and how you feel. Respectfully request the other person to help you understand, since you really would like to resolve the problem you are having. For instance, you might say something like: "I have a feeling that you might be angry about something because of the tone of your voice, although you say you aren't. I wonder if we might discuss this, so we can deal with whatever is bothering you."

Once your perception is out in the open, you have given the other person the opportunity to address underlying feelings or issues if they exist (which they usually do when you perceive a discrepancy). That allows you to deal directly with this underlying problem that is fueling the conflict, rather than letting it continue to bubble along under the surface.

The Problem of Hidden or Wrong Assumptions

It's natural to enter any interaction with certain assumptions. You assume a particular phrasing or approach will work well with someone you know, based on your past experience with that person. You assume that someone will share your kind of humor and take a comment you make as a joke. And when you say something in a conversation, you assume it's heard and understood the way you meant it. Such assumptions come naturally, and they help to facilitate the everyday flow of interpersonal reactions. Most of the time these assumptions operate unconsciously, letting you focus on the content of what the other person is doing or saying.

But sometimes your assumptions can get you in trouble. For example, a comment you make hits someone the wrong way; a joke you make falls flat because the other person doesn't share the underlying assumption on which the comment or joke was based. Also, in a more serious situation, you might assume someone has understood, believes in, or has agreed to something, when he or she has not.

Conversely, another person might make similar incorrect assumptions about you, your reaction, your plans, or beliefs. Such scenarios can lead to real conflict, all the more upsetting because it's often hard to pin down where the problem started. Whenever something important remains unclear or unsaid, it's easy to fill in the blank with a logical assumption. But since it's also dangerous, you need to learn to recognize and challenge your tendency to assume anything. And you need to be ready to make others aware of their own assumptions (in a tactful way) when they seem to have incorrect assumptions about you.

In the worst case, mistaken assumptions can become self-fulfilling prophecies. This is what happened to Jerry, an administrative assistant in a large company. He got the impression that a co-worker didn't like him, because he felt slighted by this person one day in the company cafeteria. A few days later, when his employer called him on the carpet for making personal calls and using the xerox machine for personal purposes, he suspected that co-worker of reporting him to his boss. So in turn, he decided to make things difficult for his co-worker, and engaged in some petty sabotage. He neglected to give him some messages, and gave him others incorrectly. Eventually, as this kind of activity continued, Jerry's co-worker began to feel antagonistic to Jerry because of some of the problems he experienced (such as lost phone numbers or wrong dates), and even began to wonder if perhaps Jerry was for some reason doing these things intentionally. Tensions between the two men built, until they finally led to an actual name- calling argument, leading to a long stalemated avoidance between the two men at work. In effect, Jerry's assumptions had led to the reality he believed. This situation continued until a friend, common to both, got the two men to discuss what had happened rationally and restore peace. And only then did Jerry uncover his original wrong assumptions that had escalated into this quarrel—the man had simply not seen him, and the employer's confrontation with him had come about as a result of the employer's new policy of cracking down on the personal use of office supplies; it had nothing to do with his co-worker talking against him.

There are all sorts of everyday conflicts that can arise out of misplaced assumptions. One person assumes the other is going to take care of something for a meeting, when the other person assumes the same; so the task doesn't get done. A woman suspects a friend of secretly dating her boyfriend when she isn't; as a result a friendship, and possibly the relationship with the boyfriend, are lost. A man blames another for doing an action he was only *reported* to have done; and the integrity of both men is damaged. These faulty assumptions lead not only to conflict but to loss as well.

The best way to deal with such situations is to avoid them by not jumping to conclusions or acting on the faulty assumptions that create these problems in the first place. Such a preventative strategy can help you avoid the needless worry, anger, and confusion that occurs from taking such ill-founded actions, and from trying to repair the damaged relationships afterwards. Some ways to avoid these problems include the following:

- In an uncertain or unclear interaction, ask yourself what you are assuming. Consider how much of your theory is based on *fact*, and where you are filling in the blanks. If the situation is complex, you might prefer writing down a list of all the evidence you have. Then, imagine that you are on an impartial jury listening to this. Would the evidence really convince you? How certain can you really be of your assumptions?

- If you are operating on a tentative theory, try playing the devil's advocate to question it. Consider the possibility of an alternate theory, and ask yourself if other people's behavior might make sense in that light. In short, if you have the slightest doubt about your initial assumption, challenge it by bringing it out in the open. Then, ask clear questions or gather hard evidence to support your theory.

- If possible, share your questionable assumptions with the persons who are objects of these assumptions. Get some feedback straight from the source to see if your assumptions are correct. In any case, such openness of discussion can help to clear the air. Whether your assumptions were correct or not, the discussion opens up the door to apologies, new agreements, renewed relationships, and the possibility of change for the better.

Once a conflict has begun because of faulty assumptions, the same principle applies, since you may be able to stop the problem by revealing these assumptions. The key, as before, is to bring these assumptions out in the open and find out what really is fact and what is not. Go back as far as you need to in order to get to the bottom of things. You can use the same techniques described above.

In the event you feel the basis of the conflict is the other person's faulty assumptions, you can use these techniques to help uncover and change them:

- Ask yourself if you think the other person's behavior or attitude towards you could be based on wrong assumptions about what you think, what you believe, or what you have done or will do. Consider if you have done or said anything that might have given rise to the other person's suspicions, mistrust, or lack of correct knowledge about you.

- Suggest to the other person (tactfully again) that you think there may be some area of misunderstanding which is contributing to the conflict and which you would like to clear up. Then, describe what you think the basis of the problem or faulty assumption might be and give the other person a chance to react. Be ready to explain, clarify, or apologize, and show your willingness to accept the other's explanations, clarifications, or apologies. It can be important in such a situation to give the other person a way to save face and back off, if he has made an incorrect judgment. Your goal should be simply to get him to give up the wrong assumption, not to prove him wrong. If the person senses that you are trying to prove him at fault, this could lead him to hang on to his wrong assumption as a way of saving face.

Thus, the best way to prevent or defuse a conflict is to bring assumptions (whether your's or the other person's) out in the open to discuss them. Find out what's true and not true, and smooth over any statements or actions taken resulting from those wrong assumptions. For example, when Jerry and his co-worker finally talked about what had happened between them and revealed the false assumptions leading to the conflict, they were finally able to get things patched over. Certainly, there may be a need to patch up other difficulties arising from the actions due to the false assumptions—but at least getting the assumptions out in the open by talking about them is a start.

The Problem of No Communication

Sometimes even when people appear to be speaking freely, they fail to communicate important information. It's a case of no communication if at least one person holds back true feelings, thoughts, or desires. People in this situation often feel angry or resentful when other people don't give them what they want, or act in ways they don't like. But they still don't state clearly what's bothering them. They just keep hoping people will read their minds. In another scenario, people fail to ask for clarification when they don't understand someone else's communication. This, too, is a case of no communication. It can lead people to act inappropriately or fail to act at all, and that can contribute to conflict. Since resolution rests on communication, the problem escalates as long as communication remains closed.

You can see examples of this no-communication problem all around you. For example, if you look at the advice columns in daily newspapers, you'll see this is a common complaint: "My husband doesn't talk to me … he shuts me out of his life … he doesn't share his feelings.…" "My boss is always blaming me for things, but then he doesn't tell me what he wants me to do.…" "We have relatives who barge in and stay with us for days, and I feel very resentful. I've tried to give them hints that we don't want them there by saying how much work we have with the kids, but still they come each year. What can we do?…"

In so many of these cases, the problem seems to cry out for its solution—why don't you just tell the person or persons causing the problem what you really think or feel? Don't be shy. Don't beat around the bush. Don't try to drop hints and let the other person guess. Just say it. Perhaps be diplomatic; be tactful. But say it. The neglected wife might point out how she feels shut out and how she would like to be able to understand and share with her husband. The employee might point out to his boss that he would like to get clearer instructions. The put-upon wife with relatives might simply tell the relatives that it isn't convenient for them to stay because of the pressures of the children, or perhaps they might come another time when she has less work, or perhaps if they do want to come they might be able to help out.

The key to the no-communication problem is, not surprisingly, communication. Be open; talk about whatever is hidden or unclear. (If it's hard to assess those hidden needs, refer back to the previous chapter.) Otherwise, the tensions created by the lack of communication can build into a painful stalemate. They might get siphoned off into displays of resentment or anger. Or you might spend all your energy worrying about something, or reacting to something, based on a misperception.

To avoid this no-communication problem yourself, some things you can do are the following:

- Ask yourself if you are saying what you mean. Is there anything you are saying that could be unclear or subject to misinterpretation by the other person? You might look for cues that indicate the other person may not be understanding, such as a confused, bewildered look, or a replay of a previous question or conversation that suggests the other person didn't really hear you. Then, if you think there was a communication misfire, you might slow down, back up, and explain in other words what you said. Or alternatively, you might ask the other person to state what he or she thinks you said, to see if he or she did understand. If not, you can explain again.
- Ask yourself if you are saying what you really want, need, or feel. If not, you probably won't get it. If you are talking about something that feels sensitive for you or is unpleasant to deal with, you can couch it in diplomatic language or gradually build up to it tactfully. But if you are beating around the bush too much, what you are saying won't be clear. So even if it is difficult for you, zero in on what you really want to say. You might even let the other person know you find it difficult to say this, to prepare the way for your comments.
- Ask yourself if you are understanding the other person. Are you really listening openly and receptively? Or are any assumptions, expectations, or desires of your own getting in the way? If there is any uncertainty, one helpful technique is to describe what you think you heard the other person say. Then, see if he or she agrees. If so, you can move on; if not, ask the person to explain again.

The Problem of Being Unclear

A corollary to the no-communication problem is the problem of being unclear. That can lead to as many misunderstandings about what is said or meant as no communication. Unclarity or vagueness can be tempting if your subject is an uncomfortable one. You may want to skip details if you are pressed for time.

Or you may want to use a smokescreen to avoid taking responsibility when you choose not to deal with something or hope you can pass the buck instead. You can contribute to the problem of unclarity as a listener, too. You may feel embarrassed to admit you didn't "get" something, or you may not want to slow things down or disturb the other person by suggesting something he or she said is unclear.

At the moment, a lack of clarity may prove appealing. But ultimately, the failure of communication will make itself felt. A delay in clearing things up may only make the situation worse, as more incorrect statements and wrong actions follow the initial lack of understanding. The spiral of wrongheaded responses and counterresponses can lead you into an ever-escalating conflict.

A good example of the danger of unclear communication is the boss who asks his or her employee to do something, but gives unclear instructions (or at least instructions the employee doesn't understand). The employer doesn't confirm with the employee that the instructions were clearly understood, so there is no opportunity to clear up any problems. And the employee doesn't say he is unsure about what to do (perhaps because he feels he should know the job and feels his boss will criticize him for not knowing). The result is a job done wrong. Depending on how seriously wrong it is, the mistake might lead to major conflicts, lost jobs, even lawsuits. And the fault lies both with the boss, who does not make sure important information is clearly presented and then understood, and the employee, who does not ask the boss to explain something he does not understand early on.

Likewise, personal relationships can easily disintegrate into conflict and confusion when a lack of clarity leads to misunderstandings. For example, Nora told a friend she was arriving at the airport at a certain time and asked her friend to pick her up. She gave the airline and the flight number, and it seemed like everything was perfectly arranged. But Nora had forgotten to indicate which airport. Her friend went to the airport in that city, whereas Nora arrived at another airport in a nearby city which she usually flew in and out of because there was less traffic and hassle. Neither thought to ask which airport, since each thought the airport meant was perfectly clear. The friend thought it was obvious Nora meant the city airport, while Nora thought it was obvious to her friend she would be arriving at her usual airport. The women were communicating past each other, instead of double-checking what they heard and understood to make sure everything was perfectly clear. And so each ended up waiting and angry at the other person.

There are all sorts of everyday—and not so everyday—problems triggered by the basic problem of unclear communication: missed appointments; misquotes in articles and reports; wrong specifications on a job; rumors based on wrong facts. The list goes on and on.

But again, the solution is really quite simple and obvious. If you hear something and don't understand what the person has said, wants, or means, then simply say you aren't clear. Even if you *think* you understood, it's a good idea to repeat back what you think the other means to be sure. You don't want to repeat things continually, since this will bog down the conversation. But when you do this occasionally, it helps to reassure the speaker that you are listening attentively, as well as serving as a check-point to show that you are understanding what was said (or it gives the speaker a chance to make corrections if you are not).

Alternatively, you can ask the other person to describe briefly what he or she heard you say, to be sure that what you said was understood. Do so especially if the information you conveyed is particularly important or complex. The key is to make sure that the understandings go back and forth both ways. If you do find that there has been any misunderstanding of meaning in either direction, talk about what is wrong and clarify what is unclear or incorrect. The process may sound very elementary. Yet, often people take it for granted that what they have said has been expressed clearly and understood; they don't think to question such things and go back to basics. That's where misunderstandings and conflicts can build—on a simple communication that turns out to be unclear.

So concentrate on being clear. Spell out what you mean. And look for signs that the other person understands what you are saying: such as by responding "I understand" or "I got it," and showing by replies or reactions that he or she has *really* gotten your meaning. If at times you're not sure, or when the message is very important or complex, ask the person to repeat his understanding of your message back to you, to make sure it has been gotten. And if *you* should fail to understand something the first time through, admit it. Don't worry about seeming dense or stupid. You only err if you act like you have understood something when you haven't, because then you are likely to make a mistake in the future. By acknowledging when you don't understand something, you're saving face in the long run and showing yourself to be honest and eager to get things right from the start.

Learning To Listen Well

Just as many people think they are expressing themselves well when they are not, many people don't know how to listen well. It's little wonder that attempts at communication so often go awry. Good, or "active," listening is one of the most effective communication skills you can learn. It will help you avoid all the problems described in this chapter—acting from wrong assumptions, leaving important information unclear, failing to communicate entirely—and some others as well.

Failing to listen well is a major source of conflict *beyond* the obvious reasons. Not listening can also convey an impression of hostility, bias, or critical judgment of the person who is speaking. Frowns, restlessness, and gestures of impatience can show a lack of interest, disregard, or empathy for the person speaking. That doesn't make the speaker feel too good and can create a real strain in the relationship—but it may be entirely unintended on your part.

Conversely, if you can make another person feel really listened to, acknowledged, and understood, you'll minimize your chances of conflict and ill will. You'll also profit from whatever information he or she is trying to convey. This doesn't mean you have to agree with everything the person is saying. But the person needs to feel heard and his or her communication accepted. It's the same principle as allowing an angry person to vent his or her feelings as you listen receptively—although in this case you need to pay more attention and involve yourself more fully. The ideal is to listen with empathy. You need to show that you accept what the person is saying without judgment.

You need to show that you at least understand how he or she might see things from his or her point of view, even if you don't see things the same way. Sometimes it can be hard to adopt this approach, especially in the middle of an upsetting conflict. But if you can manage to calm yourself down enough to concentrate on active listening, you will find that this approach can do wonders for resolving the conflict. It will help to calm the other person if that person is agitated and upset. It will pave the way for a clearer discussion of the conflict. And it will make you a better communicator in most of your interpersonal encounters.

According to communications experts, it's important to listen for two things when you listen attentively. First is listening for content—what's actually being said. But second, and very important, is listening for feelings. In a conflict situation, a lot of feelings can be buried under the outward message you are hearing. It's essential to bring those feelings out, if you hope for a satisfying, lasting resolution. Otherwise, unexpressed hostilities can fester, such as in the case of a spouse who finally says "fine, fine, do that," just to end the argument. Yet, he or she is still seething underneath. The external argument may be over, but the internal conflict is still going on, and it will heat up again.

If you are in a situation where someone has these underlying negative feelings, chances are you'll sense anger or resentment when it's contained in the person's voice. You may want to overlook those perceptions to maintain an outward calm. But the best approach is to acknowledge those feelings you sense. You might even refer to these unvocalized feelings, so you can work on truly clearing the air. One way to do this is to say something to suggest what you think the other person may be feeling underneath, such as: "I sense that …" or "It sounds like…" Then, add your interpretation: "you may be feeling [and you fill in the blank] _____." This way, by gently suggesting what you perceive (not by trying to impose your interpretation on the other person with a comment like: "you must be feeling"), the other person knows you are just checking, not presuming, and can sense your concern to resolve the problem, not just get it out of the way. Then, he or she can let you know if you are correct about these unresolved feelings, and he or she will feel heard and understood. Once true feelings are out in the open, or consciously set aside after being expressed, you are more likely to achieve a mutual, more deeply satisfying resolution.

For example, suppose you hear someone say something that suggests he or she isn't saying what he or she really means. You might come back with a question or observation that shows you are really concerned and gives that person permission to state his or her real feelings or concerns. The following chart illustrates how you might go about interpreting and responding to the meanings you sense from what someone says.

What the Person Says	What You Think He or She Means or Feels	What You Might Say to Bring Out Real Meanings or Feelings
"Do what you want."	"I don't like what you want to do, but I don't feel like you care about what I think. I feel like you are going to do it your way anyway."	"I feel like you may not *really* want this. What do you really want, and can we talk about this?"
"I don't care."	"I do care, but I feel frustrated. You aren't listening to what I am saying."	"But you do seem to be annoyed by what happened, and I am concerned about how you feel."
"Have it your way."	"I'm too tired to struggle with you anymore. Do what you want, but I don't like it."	"But I'd like to be sure I have your input and agreement, too. What would you like to see happen, so we can both get what we want?"

| "Fine," or any other words of apparent approval, that are spoken in a reluctant or angry tone of voice. | "It's not fine, and I'm really very angry with you. I feel like I'm being pushed around." | "But it sounds like it really isn't fine for you. What do you *really* feel about this? I'd really like to know." |

Thus keep in mind that listening for *real* feelings is one of the key principles of listening well. The other principles are outlined below.

- *Listen with empathy.* Regardless of how wronged or hostile you may feel, disengage yourself from your own feelings, and listen with an open, receptive mind. Try to put yourself in the place of the other person. Picture how the situation looks from his or her perspective. Imagine how *you* and your responses sound from the other's point of view.

- *Focus on the issues.* Don't let yourself get sidetracked by responding to the person's personality. Remind yourself to listen to what the person is saying about the particular issue involved in the dispute. If the conversation strays, you can ask questions to get the conversation back on track.

- *Show positive regard and respect for the other person.* Whatever the person says, remind yourself that you will show you respect what that person is saying and feeling. Likewise, remind yourself that you will not get sucked into name calling or other shows of disrespect. Instead, you will emphasize the need to listen to and respect one another. If the person you are having an argument with says something like: "You really are a jerk," try to respond with understanding and empathy to his or her underlying feelings. Acknowledge his or her anger or frustration. Get the discussion back to the issues by saying something like: "It sounds like this situation is really upsetting to you. What would you like to do about it?" You might also remind the person about the need to deal with each other with respect by saying something like: "I know you're angry, but let's try not to call each other names, and let's work on solving this problem." In other words, take the high ground as you listen to try to keep emotions under control. Then, as soon as you can, get back to dealing constructively with the problem.

- *Listen attentively without judgment.* This is the best way to get the other person to say what he or she really thinks, and let out any feelings that might be standing in the way of working out the problem. It allows the other person to "blow off steam." One way to do this is simply to nod from time to time. You can offer occasional responses like "uh-huh," or comments like: "Then what happened?" or "How did you feel?" Such gestures and questions show that you're paying attention. They also help create an open, non-judgmental environment where the other person feels free to express what he or she really thinks. Ideally, by modeling attentive, non-judgmental listening yourself, you'll be able to encourage someone else to do the same. That will go a long way toward creating the receptive environment you need to come up with a productive solution to a conflict.

- *Reflect back what you think you heard to show the other person you're really listening.* Use your own words to repeat important points the other person is making. You might also reflect back what you think the other person is feeling. The idea is to be a kind of mirror to the other person to show you are really listening and understanding. Yet, you're not just parroting back the words. You are paraphrasing what the person said, and you are presenting your perception of the other's feelings. This clarifies that person's message in your own mind—and ensures you're not mis-hearing, because you give the other person a chance to correct you if you have heard anything wrong.

  In paraphrasing, you might begin by saying something like: "Let me see if I understand what you just said," or "Am I correct in thinking that you're saying … ?" Then, you restate what you just heard in other words. If you are reflecting the other person's feelings, you might say something like, "You sound [angry, upset, confused …] about [identify the situation]." Be careful not to sound too definite or sure of yourself in reading feelings ("you are confused"). To do so is to lay your own assumptions or

perceptions on the other person. Rather, say, "You seem …
about…." A sympathetic, interpretive comment can be
particularly useful when someone seems very upset. It
helps the other person know his or her emotion has reg-
istered with you, even though it was expressed through a
confusion of words and feelings. When you say something
like:"It looks like you are really angry about that," or "It
seems like that experience was really painful for you,"
assuming your perception is accurate, the other person can
feel your concern and understanding. It may even help the
person clarify his own uncertain feelings for himself. That
helps break down communication barriers. It also em-
phasizes caring over hostility.

- *Clarify what you don't understand or are unsure about.* This
  point is important enough to have warranted its own
  section earlier in this chapter. It is an integral part of
  effective listening. The key here is to get more information
  if there are facts you don't understand or if you are uncertain about what the other person really means or feels. This
  principle may sound obvious, but often people go on in
  conversations without filling in these gaps. Then misunderstandings can build and build. For instance, say
  things like: "Do you mean that [fill in what you think is
  meant]?" "Are you feeling [upset, angry, discouraged]?"
  "Could you explain a little more about what you say
  happened?" "I don't understand what you just said."
- *Encourage further discussion.* If you feel the other person
  hasn't fully explained the situation, his point of view, or
  his feelings, you might encourage the person to say a little
  bit more. A good way to do this is with open-ended
  comments. You might say something like: "Could you say
  more about this?" "Tell me more about it," "How did
  you feel when …?" or "Can you tell me why this is so
  important to you?" When you ask such things, be sure to
  express your question in a neutral way to encourage the
  person to open up. You want to avoid a challenging tone,
  implying that you are questioning the person's reasons for
  feeling or responding a certain way. That approach is apt
  to put the person on the defensive. The idea is to pave the
  way for more discussion in both your question and your
  tone.

- *Use non-verbal listening responses to encourage the other person to continue talking.* Smile if you can, lean towards the speaker, nod, use eye contact. And say things like "uh-huh" to show you are listening and are receptive.

Remember, the goal is to show you hear and understand the other person, and care what he or she is saying. It might feel uncomfortable or insincere at first to repeatedly express what you are hearing and understanding. But you'll find that with practice this approach comes naturally. And if you take it seriously, you'll find that your increased concern for the other person and his or her satisfaction becomes genuine.

Expressing Your Own Feelings and Needs in a Non-Threatening Way

You can use your good communication skills to tone down the emotional level of a conflict, to find out what the other person wants, and to promote the open receptive climate that encourages conflict resolution. You can also draw on these skills to put forth your *own* feelings and needs. And you can do so in a way that reduces the chances for escalation—or even initiation—of a conflict.

One key way of doing this is through using what are called "I statements" or "I messages." Essentially, this is a way of giving someone else information about your own needs, feelings, or opinions in a non-threatening, non-judgmental way. You say what *you* want, think, or need, not what the other person needs to do or say. You are asserting yourself, yet not putting pressure on the other person at the same time. That way the other person doesn't feel blamed, judged, or attacked; the person won't feel cornered or respond defensively, thereby starting or upping the conflict.

"I statements," simply, start with "I" and express a personal feeling or reaction. For example, if you feel a need for more time to respond to what the other person wants, you might say: *"I would like some more time to think that over."* Or if you have a difference of opinion with the other person, you might say something like: *"I don't agree with you about that, and I would like to explain my own feelings about the matter."* If you would like the other person to do something for you, you might comment in a neutral, requesting fashion: *"I would appreciate it if you could do that for me as soon as possible."*

By contrast, "you statements" or "you messages" can stir up conflicts because they can make it sound like you are blaming, judging, or attacking the other person, thus triggering a defensive response. Typical "you statements" include: "You're wrong," "You should do such and such," "You're inconsiderate," "You always do ..."

One major problem with "you statements" is that they make it seem like the person giving them is right and the other person is wrong. In fact, they really express a difference of opinion or the point of view of the person making the statement. The way they are expressed, they can readily make the "you" feel angry, and usually defensive. The person can feel accused or blamed and thus feel a need to explain or defend himself against the remark. He (or she) may feel irate that the other person feels righteous or justified enough to make such a remark. The conflict is then not only about the original problem, but about the attitude of the person making the "you statements." The situation gets worse instead of better.

A perfect example of this is the parent-child situation in which the parent is angry at the child for having done something wrong, such as leaving a messy room. Instead of asking the child to clean up the room, or providing some incentive so the child will keep the room clean in the future, the parent says something like: "You always leave the room a mess." Well, now the conflict is no longer just about the room. It's about what the child does and why, and about whether the child always does it, or just sometimes. And the conflict will make the child feel bad—and resentful.

Similarly, couples often get into this "you statement" behavior. They throw accusations at each other about something ("You never take out the garbage," "Why can't you be like ... and do ...") rather than focus on the issue at hand ("Could we work out some arrangement about who takes out the garbage? Could you take it out on ...?" or "I like it when you do ...").

If you couch these "you statements" expressing what you want from the other person in a more neutral way, using the "I message" to soften them, you are more likely to make positive, productive contact. The other person is better able to listen and respond, without feeling confronted by a demand, blame, or threat.

Some examples of how you can turn these accusing-sounding "you statements" into more productive, communicative "I statements" are the following:

You Statements	I Statements
Accusatory:	Expressing Feelings, Requests, and Solution-Oriented:
"*You* never call me until the last minute to do something."	"When you call me to make plans at the last minute, *I'm not always free* to do something with you, although *I would* like to do something if I could. I sometimes feel hurt that you wait so long to call. *I would appreciate it* if you could call me a little earlier about arrangements in the future if you can."
"Why do you always have to interrupt?"	"When you try to talk to me while I'm talking, *I can't really pay attention* to what you're trying to say, because I'm thinking about something else. So I'd appreciate it if you could wait until I'm finished talking, unless it is really important and you feel you have to interrupt right away."
"You don't respect me. You never remember my birthday."	"When you don't remember my birthday, I feel like you don't care about or respect me. I would like to feel that you care."
"You are annoying me with all your questions."	"When you ask me questions while I'm doing something else, I feel distracted and irritated, because I'm not really ready to pay attention to them. I'd appreciate it if you could ask me these questions again at a more convenient time, such as [you specify when]."

"You never do what I want; always what you want."

"When you make a decision for us without asking for my opinion, I feel hurt and I feel that you aren't interested in my ideas. I'd like it if we could discuss these things so we could do what we both want."

The basic model for these more complex "I messages" is to begin with a neutral, non-blameful description of the other's behavior that disturbs you. Explain your rational and emotional reactions to this behavior. Explain why this behavior is a problem for you, or simply describe the effects on you of this behavior. And finally, state in very gentle, assertive but not aggressive terms what you would like to see happen. Use words like "I would like," "I would appreciate," or "I would prefer."

The "I message" model, spelled out, looks something like this:

When you (non-blameful description of the other's behavior), I feel (your feelings or emotions about his behavior) because (why his or her behavior is a problem for you or its effects on you), and I would like, appreciate, prefer, etc. (what you want to happen).

Summing Up—The Keys To Communicating to Conquer Conflict

The way you communicate—and set the stage to help others communicate—can go a long way toward avoiding a conflict or dissipating one once it gets going. The basic keys include the following:

- Pay attention to non-verbal cues that suggest a discrepancy between what the speaker is thinking or feeling and what he or she is saying. Bring these issues out in the open.
- Watch for hidden or wrong assumptions—your own or the other person's. Bring them out in the open so mistakes can be corrected.

- Work towards open channels of communication. Say what you think or feel diplomatically, and encourage the other party to open up and talk to you, too.
- Avoid unclarity. If something is unclear to you, ask for clarification so you understand. And if someone else seems unclear, check this out and then provide the necessary explanations yourself.
- Learn to listen well. Do so with interest and concern and respect. You want to show empathy, and to indicate that the speaker is being heard and understood. Also, listen attentively without interruption or judgment. From time to time reflect back what you heard to show the other person you're following the conversation.
- Express your own feelings and needs in a non-threatening way, using "I statements." Avoid "you statements," which can make the other person feel judged, put down, or blamed.

7

Choosing a Style of Handling Conflicts To Suit the Conflict Situation

When you are in a conflict situation, one way to better deal with it is to recognize that you can choose among different styles of handling conflicts based on your own personal style, the style of others involved in the conflict, and the nature of the conflict itself. The following chapter is designed to help you recognize these styles and learn when to best apply them, so you can choose the best strategies for you in different situations.

Recognizing the Styles of Handling Conflict

There are five major styles of handling conflict. These have been described and used extensively in educational and business management programs based on a system called the Thomas-Kilmann Conflict Mode Instrument.[1] The system creates a profile of each individual's usual style or approach to dealing with conflict. The major conflict styles are derived from the common roots of all conflict: an incompatibility between the concerns of two or more parties.

---

[1] The Thomas-Kilmann Conflict Mode Instrument was developed by Kenneth W. Thomas and Ralph H. Kilmann in 1972. "Mode" is short for "Management of Differences Exercise."

Your style in dealing with a particular conflict depends on the degree to which you attempt to satisfy your own concern (by acting either unassertively or assertively) and to satisfy the other party's concern (by acting cooperatively or uncooperatively). When you put these two considerations together, they can form a grid. This is Thomas and Kilmann's method of identifying and labeling the five major styles of handling conflict.

The Conflict Handling Styles Grid

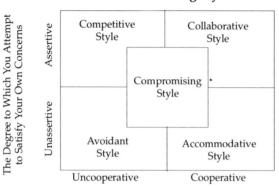

The Degree to Which You Attempt
to Satisfy Other's Concerns

The grid can be used to identify your style or anyone else's style. Begin by looking at the side of the grid labeled "unassertive" and "assertive." If your reaction is unassertive, you will tend to pull back from the conflict; whereas if your reaction is assertive, you'll be more aggressive and active in dealing with it. These are qualities you can recognize in others and recognize and control in yourself.

The top side of the grid deals with cooperation. If you are cooperative, you'll try to work along with the person or the group you are having a conflict with. If you are uncooperative, you'll seek to resolve the issue in your own way or not deal with the issue at all. The degree of cooperation offered should also be readily identifiable in yourself and others.

When you put these two sides of the grid together, you get a matrix of the five styles with the compromising style in the middle. This represents a balance of being cooperative and uncooperative, unassertive and assertive. As you look more closely at these different styles, you may recognize one or another as the more usual ways you tend to deal with a conflict yourself; and you may find that other people you relate to also have certain styles they tend to use. Then, too, under certain conditions you may be more likely to use one style rather than another. Everyone might try all the styles at some point, although people have certain style preferences. Certain styles might also be more appropriate and more effective in resolving particular types of conflict. Each style is described briefly below; ways of applying each style are discussed at the end of the chapter.

The Competitive Style

As the grid shows, a person who uses a competitive style is very assertive and interested in getting his or her own way. He or she isn't particularly interested in cooperating with other people, but instead approaches the conflict in a very forceful way. The rationale might go: "I don't care what other people think. I'm going to make sure I get my own way." Or as Thomas and Kilmann describe the dynamic, you strive primarily to satisfy your concern at the expense of others, by forcing people to do it your way, arguing, and pulling rank. You use your power to win your objective; and if you have enough power, you can often do that.

This can be a good style to use if you are in a position of power; you know your idea or approach is right for the situation, and you are able to prevail over others. However, it's probably not the kind of approach you'd want to use in personal relations; you want to get along with people, but the competitive style can alienate people. And if you use the competitive style when you don't have a lot of power in a situation, such as in a disagreement with your boss over some matter, you might get yourself fired.

More specifically, some of the times when this is a good style to use are when:

- the issue is very important to you, and you have a big stake in getting your way;

- you have authority to make the decision, and it seems clear that this is the one best way;
- a decision has to be made quickly, and you have the power to make it;
- you feel you have no other options and you have nothing to lose;
- you are in an emergency situation where immediate decisive action is necessary;
- you can't get a group to agree, feel you are at an impasse, and someone must make the group move ahead;
- you have to make an unpopular decision, but action is required now, and you have the power to make that choice.

You may not be particularly popular when you use this approach, although you may win admirers if your solution works. But then this isn't the style to use if being popular and well-liked is your primary objective; rather you'll use it to get your way in something that is important to you, when you feel you must act quickly to get your way immediately, and when you feel confident you will win, because you have the power or position to do so.

The Avoidant Style

The second major approach occurs when you don't assert yourself, don't cooperate, or avoid the conflict entirely. This is the approach you might choose when the problem situation is not that important to you, when you don't want to be hassled about it, or when you feel you are in a no-win situation. You might also act in an avoidant style when you feel you are wrong and the other person is right, or when the other person has more power. These are all good reasons to decide it's not worth standing up for your position in a conflict. You might try changing the subject, walking out of the room, or doing something to put the conflict aside or delay it. You might think: "I'm not going to deal with this matter now." In short, you don't attempt to satisfy either your or the other's concern. Instead, you sidestep the issue by ignoring it, passing the buck, delaying, or using other tactics.

This avoidance can be a good approach to use if you're faced with dealing with a difficult person, and there is no strong reason to *have* to be or work together. The approach can also be useful if you are trying to make a decision, are unsure about what to do, and don't have to make that decision immediately. Instead of getting tense about trying to resolve the situation right away, you might allow yourself the luxury of extra time, and consciously avoid deciding for the present. You just need to make sure you *do* come back to the issue eventually; otherwise, this approach can look like procrastination or irresponsibility. Another good time to use the avoidant style is when you feel you don't have enough information to resolve a particular situation. If you have the option of waiting, and time might provide the answer, it may be best to acknowledge that, and say, "I can't deal with this now; I'll wait."

Below are more specific situations where you might want to use the avoidant style.

- tensions are too high, and you feel a need to cool down
- the issue isn't very important to you or you feel it's objectively a trivial issue that's not worth dealing with
- you're having a bad day, and there's a good chance you might get upset or not deal with the issue properly
- you know you can't, or probably won't, win in the conflict
- you want to buy more time, perhaps because you need to get more information or get some assistance from others
- the situation is complex and difficult to change, so you feel tackling it will just be a wasted effort
- you have little power to resolve the situation or to get it resolved in a desirable way
- you feel that others have a better chance of resolving the situation
- there's danger in trying to deal with the situation at the moment, since bringing the conflict out into the open might make the situation worse

Though some people may think of avoidance as "running away" from the issue rather than a valid conflict-managing technique, in fact evasion or delay can be an appropriate and constructive response to a problem situation. Perhaps if you try to ignore it, say nothing, leave, drop the subject, or shift attention to something else, the conflict will resolve itself. If not, you can deal with it later when you feel more up to it.

The Accommodative Style

The third style is accommodative. This occurs in the case where you work cooperatively with the other person, without trying to assert your own concerns. You might take this approach when the outcome of the situation is very important to the other person but of less importance to you. Also, you might be accommodative when you feel you can't win because the other person has more power; you just give in and go along with what the other person wants. Thomas and Kilmann describe this style by saying that when you accommodate, you sacrifice your own concern in order to satisfy another's concern by conceding, taking pity on that person, or otherwise giving in.

Since you are putting your own concerns aside in using this approach, it's most appropriate to do this when you don't have a lot invested in a situation or a lot at stake in the outcome. That lets you feel comfortable going along with what the other person wants. After all, you don't want to accommodate somebody in a case where you'll feel resentful. If you feel you'd be giving up something that is important to you, and you don't feel good about that, the accommodative style is probably not appropriate. The same might be true if you feel the other person hasn't given up enough in return or doesn't appreciate what you have given. It's the type of approach to use when you feel like you are not losing too much by giving something up. Or you might try using this strategy to smooth things over for the time being, and plan to raise the subject again, with the goal of achieving an outcome more in line with your desired position later.

Accommodation can be a little bit like avoidance, since you can use it to delay finding a true resolution to a problem. But the key difference is that in accommodation you cooperate; you address the situation and agree to do what the other person wants. When you use avoidance, you don't do anything to further the other person's desires, and decide something only by default, if at all. You just push the situation away.

More specifically, some of the best times to consider accommodating are these.

- when you don't really care that much what happens

- when you want to keep the peace and maintain harmony with others
- when you feel it is more important to maintain a relationship with someone than to get the matter decided your way
- when you recognize that the outcome is much more important to the other person than to you
- when you recognize that you are wrong and the other person is right
- when you have little power or little chance of winning
- when you think the other person might learn from the situation if you go along with what he wants, even though you don't agree with what he is doing or think he is making a mistake

By giving in, agreeing, or sacrificing your own concerns to what the other person wants, you may be able to smooth over a bad situation and restore harmony. You might then continue to go along with this outcome, if it feels all right to you. Or you might use this period of smoothing things over as a way to gain time, so you can work on finding a final resolution you would prefer.

The Collaborative Style

The fourth style is the collaborative approach. In this approach, you get actively involved in working out a conflict by asserting what you want, while still trying to cooperate with the other person. This style can take a little longer to work through than most other ways of handling conflict, since you first want to get all of the issues and concerns you both have on the table, and then you want to listen to each other's needs. But if you have the time and the issue is important enough, this is a good way to find a win-win situation that satisfies the needs of both.

This style works particularly well when the parties have different underlying needs. In such cases, the source of dissatisfaction may be hard to pin down. It may appear initially that both want the same thing or have opposing long-term goals, which are the immediate source of conflict. However, often there is a difference between the surface issues or positions in dispute and the underlying interests or needs, which are the real sources of conflict.

For example, the surface issue creating a conflict at work may be an employee's lateness. But that lateness may only mask a deeper conflict, in that the man is dissatisfied with his work— he feels a lack of respect, acknowledgment, or responsibility, and he is responding by a growing disconnection from his work. If only the surface issue is dealt with, this will only result in a superficial treatment that is likely not to have long-term effectiveness, because the roots of the problem still remain. The man might stop being late, but then he might engage in some unconscious or not-so-unconscious sabotage acts at work, take some extra breaktime for himself, or help himself to office facilities or supplies, telling himself he deserves them because he is underpaid and under-appreciated. That would be his own way of making up some extra compensation to himself. By contrast, using a collaborative approach encourages each person to bring all of his true needs and desires into the open, so they can be addressed. The man in the above situation might point out that he feels a need for more recognition, appreciation, and responsibility. If the boss understands this, he might be willing to offer more, resulting in the man becoming more committed to his work again—and thereby ending the lateness problem, as well as having other positive effects.

Thus, the key to a successful collaboration involves taking the time to look at underlying interests and needs, in the hopes of finding some way of meeting the real needs of both parties. Together you might search for new alternatives or work out good compromises once you both understand all the issues.

More specifically, this approach can be a good one to use under the following conditions.

- when the issues are very important to both or all parties, and no one is willing to let go entirely
- when you have a close, continuing, or interdependent relationship with the other party
- when you have the time to deal with the problem (this is a good approach for a conflicts arising in a long-term project)
- when both you and the other party are aware of the problem and are clear about what you want

- when both you and the other party are willing to put some thought and work into finding a solution
- when you both have the skills to articulate your concerns and to listen to what others have to say
- when you and others in the conflict have a similar amount of power, or are willing to put aside any power differences in order to work together as equals in coming up with a solution

Collaboration is an amicable, thoughtful approach towards getting everyone's needs recognized and met. However, it takes a certain amount of work and effort. All parties have to make a commitment in time, and they have to be able to clarify their wants, express their needs, listen to others do the same, and then explore alternatives and agree to solutions. Without any one of these elements, this approach won't work. Collaboration is thus more complicated than other approaches, but it can afford the most mutually satisfying resolution to a serious and important conflict.

The Compromising Style

In the center of the matrix is the compromise-sharing approach. You give up a little bit of what you want to get the rest of what you want, and the other parties in the conflict do the same. Or in Thomas-Kilmann terms, you settle for a partial satisfaction of your concern and a partial satisfaction of the other's concern. You do this by making exchanges and concessions, and bargaining to come up with a compromise solution you each can agree to.

To some extent, such acts may sound like collaboration. But compromise occurs on a more superficial level than collaboration; you give up something, the other person gives up something, and eventually you come to a resolution. You are not searching for underlying needs and interests as in collaboration. You are dealing only with what people say they want.

A compromise approach might be especially appropriate when you and another person want the same thing, and you know you both can't end up getting it. For instance, you both want the same office, or you want to spend the same vacation time doing something different. So you work out a compromise based on sharing by giving up a little bit of what you each want to do. Thus, in the office case, you might work out something like: "You take the office for four hours and then I'll take the office for four hours," or in the vacation case, your compromise might be something like: "Well, we'll go to the mountains for part of the vacation, if you're willing to go to the beach for the other part."

The difference in the collaborative approach is that you would search for the underlying needs and attempt to work out an arrangement based on that. For instance, in discussing the office, you might come to realize that your need really isn't for that particular office; you really want the recognition that goes with it, and you can get that recognition in other, more important ways. You might get some extra secretarial help from the secretarial pool and access to a larger conference room. Or you might get more time off from the job. In collaborating, your focus is on resolving underlying issues and needs; in a compromise you deal with the conflict situation as a given and look for ways to influence or alter those givens through giving in or making exchanges. The goal of collaboration is a long-term win-win solution; in compromise the outcome may be more short-term and expedient. At the end of a successful compromise, a person might agree with the attitude: "I can live with that." The emphasis is not on win-win, but on "We can't both get what we want, so let's work out something we can both live with."

In such situations, a collaboration may not even be possible. Perhaps neither of you has the time or the energy to devote to it, or you have mutually exclusive goals. A compromise would be the best way to go.

More specifically, some of the times when a compromise is most appropriate are the following:

- when you have the same amount of power as someone else and you are both committed to mutually exclusive goals
- when you want to achieve a resolution quickly, because of time pressures or because it's more economical and efficient that way
- when you can settle for a temporary resolution
- when you will benefit from a short-term gain

- when you haven't been able to work out a solution through either collaboration or a more competitive/forceful approach, and compromise alone offers *some* solution
- when the goals are not extremely important to you, and you are willing to modify your objectives
- when a compromise will make a relationship or agreement work, and you'd rather have that than nothing at all

Compromise is often a good fallback or last resort approach to achieving a resolution. You might even choose it from the start when you don't have the power to get what you want, can't work out a collaboration, and neither want to give in nor avoid the issue. This way, at least you can get part of your agenda met while the other party gets part of his—and you can always try another conflict handling approach later if your initial compromise doesn't seem to provide the long-term answer.

When you do seek a compromise with someone, you should start by clarifying your respective wants and needs. Then look for areas of agreement. You should make suggestions and listen to what the other person suggests, and be ready to make offers, exchanges and bargains. Negotiate until you are able to find some mutually agreeable formula on what each of you will give up and get in return. Ideally, you'll both be satisfied with the compromise.

Recognizing Your Own Approach to Conflict

It is important to recognize that all of these styles of conflict are appropriate at different times, and no one style is better than another. Optimally, you should be able to use any of these styles effectively, and consciously choose when it is best to use each one. The best approach will depend on the particular factors in each situation, and also on what feels most comfortable to you. It's natural to prefer certain styles over others, but strict style preferences may limit you: you may avoid or mishandle the most appropriate style for a particular conflict. Thus, it's important to be aware of your own style preferences, as well as the range of alternatives. This puts you in a better position to make choices in handling conflict situations.

If you notice that you are likely to avoid using a particular style or don't feel comfortable or competent using it, you might work on developing your ability to use that style. For example, if you feel you tend to accommodate others too much rather than stick up for your own position, you might work on being more assertive and forceful. That way you can use the competitive style when the situation warrants. Or if you feel you compromise too much because you are impatient, maybe you can learn to slow down in handling important issues, since sometimes patient collaboration will help you find a better solution.

The first step is to assess your usual style of approaching conflict. Chances are you tend to use one or two modes most commonly, just as a performer has a characteristic style or repertoire he or she usually performs. In some cases, you may have one style that is especially predominant—your primary approach—and other styles you use commonly but less often: your secondary or tertiary styles. You might even have two equally characteristic styles—accommodation and avoidance, say, since you'll do anything to prevent a conflict—and then you would be considered "bimodal." Should you have three characteristic styles—such as fight, flight, or compromise—you would be called "trimodal."

Thomas and Kilmann developed a test they call the Conflict Mode Instrument, which is designed to give each individual a profile of scores showing him how he responds to conflict. They developed the test by questioning groups of managers. Those answers became a baseline against which to measure everyone else; when you take the test, your responses are scored relative to the managers in each conflict style or modality.

Taking this test can be very helpful in giving you some insight into yourself. Chances are you have a sense of your preferred styles, but the test will help you look at your approach very objectively by examining your reactions to a wide range of situations. When I first took the test myself with a group of managers in the non-profit sector, most of us were fairly accurate in assessing our habitual ways of dealing with conflict. The test provided confirmation, in addition to more details on your overall pattern of response. When I took the test, I found I was relatively high in competing, avoiding, and compromising, but fairly low in collaborating and accommodating. I had sensed that this would be likely in advance, since I like to reach a decision quickly, focus on getting those things I really want, and don't feel most issues are important enough to fight for my way. But the test helped me realize how much I had to gain from learning to collaborate, and introducing my needs into negotiation. Likewise, others had a sense of how they might score in advance, and found the test helped them understand more about patterns they recognized in their everyday lives. When I took the test again later, feeling more aggressive and assertive, I was indeed even higher in competition and compromise. The test reflected my own changes over time.

By the same token, you can actually take the test yourself or give yourself a quick overall assessment by thinking about the five styles, and asking yourself some questions about your use of each one. Then, you can rate yourself on which you think you use most, use best, use least, and feel most comfortable using. Chart I on the next page will help you organize your responses. As you go through this process, write down the first response that comes into mind; this is usually the most accurate, because it is the most spontaneous and the most intuitive. Also, in responding, don't try to think of how you responded to the latest conflict situation you were in or the most dramatic. Rather, review the way you have responded to conflict situations *generally* over the years. And don't try to think of the way you would like to respond—there is no right or wrong way to respond; it all depends on the situation.

You can always choose to expand your repertoire of conflict responses in the future, based on your attitudes about how you have been responding. But for now, just give your intial reaction to how you usually respond to conflict situations. The chart should give you an overall picture of how you are most and least likely to respond, and how you feel about using these different methods.

Rank what you consider your usual style of responding to conflict from 1 (high) to 5 (low) in each column based on how much you think you use that style in dealing with most conflict situations you encounter. If you feel unsure about a ranking, consider the ranking a tie. Then, skip to the next appropriate number for the following rank. (i.e.: If two styles tie for first place in a category, the third style will be given the number 3 for third). (As an example of how this ranking system works, under "Use the Most," a ranking might look something like this: Competitive 2, Avoidant 5, Accommodative 3, Collaborative 4, Compromising 1.)

Chart I: How I Usually Respond to Conflict Situations

Conflict style   **Method of use and attitude towards using**

	Use the Most	Like Using the Most	Use the Least	Feel the Least Comfortable Using
Competitive (I actively seek to get my own way)				
Avoidant (I seek to avoid the conflict situation)				
Accommodative (I seek to work out a mutually satisfying solution with others)				
Collaborative (I seek to work out a mutually satisfying solution with others)				
Compromising (I seek to work out a solution in which we each give up a little to get some of what we want)				

Assessing Your Approach to Conflict

Now that you have a clearer picture of how you generally deal with conflict, you can consider how well you feel about using that approach and whether you might benefit from developing your ability to use other styles. To do this, think back to particular conflict situations you have been in and consider what styles you have used. In some situations, you may have used several different approaches.

Then, look at the outcome for each of these situations. Was your approach to the conflict effective? Did you get what you wanted? Did the other party? Do you feel the approach you used helped achieve a favorable result? Or do you feel your approach didn't work? If so, what approach do you feel you might have used with a better result?

For example, if you tend to be a highly competitive person in your approach to conflict, that means you usually push to get your own way, and you like to see things happen quickly. At times when you are in a power position and can push things through, this approach may work. You may get other people to agree with you and do what you want.

But sometimes, even though you get outward agreement, you might notice that this approach results in negative spinoffs. Maybe people resent you and try getting back at you in other ways, through gossip or sabotage.

You might also notice other times when this approach hasn't worked from the outset. Perhaps it has led other competitive people to resist you and fight for what they want as well.

Similarly, if you tend to avoid issues, look at how well that approach has worked for you. Do you feel comfortable at having put many conflict questions on the table or out of sight? Or do you regret not having achieved a solution?

If you tend to accommodate, ask whether giving in has generally worked well for you. Do you feel okay about supporting what the other person wants to do? Or do you feel any anger or resentment when your needs remain unmet?

Likewise, as a person who tends to compromise or collaborate, ask your own set of questions to see if you have been generally effective in using that style, or whether some other approach might have been more useful. As a compromiser, you might notice if your interest in expedience is getting in your way of finding a better, more enduring solution. As a collaborator, consider if you might be spending more time than necessary in resolving your conflicts.

The point of this exercise is to remind yourself that there are numerous ways to approach any conflict, all of which can be useful to you. You may already be using all of them, though you may not be consciously planning where, when, or how best to use them. Your more usual approaches to conflict may be fine in many cases. But in other cases, it may be better to use a different approach. Reviewing past conflict experiences can help you see how well your current styles are working for you (and for others you encounter). You may find you need to be more open to using other approaches. If so, you can begin developing the ability to use them right now, so you can consciously draw on any approach for managing conflicts in the future.

The exercise on the next page will help you pinpoint particular areas of weakness where you need to develop the use of a style a little more. Also, it will help you to be more aware of the way you make choices and respond in conflict situations, so you can deal better with conflicts in the future. By being aware, you can choose if this is really the response you want to make. Also, you will develop a sense of objectivity, so you can stand back from yourself when you are involved in a conflict situation, and choose rationally what you want to do.

In Chart II, list some of the major conflict situations you have experienced; note the conflict style or styles you have used; rate each style's overall effectiveness in that situation; and note what you feel was the result of using that style, whether favorable or unfavorable. Finally, note what other approach (or approaches) you might have used with a better result. (Really picture going through with another style: What would you have said? What are the likely reactions of others and yourself? How would that relationship work differently now?)

Conflict Situation	Style Used	Overall Effectiveness (-3 to +3)	Result of Using that Style (describe benefits or negative outcomes)	Alternate Approach	Why Better

Chart II: Assessing the Effectiveness of My Use of Conflict Handling Styles

8

Choosing the Best Conflict Style in Everyday Life

The conflict handling styles described in the last chapter provide a framework for looking at how you deal with conflict and choosing the most appropriate style. This chapter is designed to look more closely at specific applications of choosing and using these styles to help you make better choices yourself.

Assessing the Balance of Power

Two key considerations in choosing an effective conflict style are the other person's position of power, relative to yours, and that person's perspective (or "where that person is coming from").

If you have more power than the other person, you may be able to use a competitive style and come on forcefully to get what you want. You can get the other person to give in (that is, to accommodate you). But if the other person has more power than you and comes on strong, you may need to be the one to accommodate. If you do try to compromise in a situation of unequal power, recognize that this power differential plays a key role in the outcome of the conflict. For unless the person with more power agrees to put position considerations aside, whoever has more power usually ends up with a better deal in the compromise. That person simply has the bargaining chips to get more of what he or she wants.

Of course, the particular situation should also affect your response when someone else has a lot of power. If you are dealing with a high-powered person who is coming on very strong, it may not work very well if you come on strong yourself: you will probably just end up butting heads. You need to think about how much you want your own goal, and whether or not you can win in the power struggle that results. If you feel that what you want is important enough, perhaps you can pull together the support of others to counteract that person's high level of power, or even tough it out on your own. But if you feel you are in a no-win situation, or that there's a great risk of being on the losing end of an out-and-out conflict, you may need to accommodate the other person and pull back. This is especially true if your potential loss is high: your job, or a friend, or a co-worker's respect.

Even if there is no power differential, but the other person feels very strongly about something, you may choose to pull back. If your valued friend has certain ideas that you disagree with, for instance, it may be better to go along with him at times, rather than force a challenge. You can avert a major blowup, and demonstrate the respect you have for that friend and that relationship.

The other person's perspective can be particularly important if you are trying to collaborate or work out a fair compromise. To achieve success in either, you both have to be on a relatively equal level of power or be willing to put power considerations aside. But that alone isn't enough. You also need to be dealing with someone who is willing to meet and discuss things with you in a good-willed way. If this is not the case, the other person may try to take advantage of you as you show signs of giving in. Then you may find your own attempts to collaborate or compromise pushed aside by the other person's more forceful competitive spirit, seeking to pressure you into accommodations. Thus you both need to proceed in good faith for collaboration or compromise to work well. If you feel the other person does not share your commitment to using either approach, it may not be appropriate for you to use that particular style.

The ideal is to aim for fairness and a good-faith approach to settling a conflict. But you'll also want to recognize those situations where you can't achieve this goal, because power or perspective differences leave you vulnerable to a competitive or an exploitive person. In such cases, it's best to acknowledge the differences early on and choose a more self-protective approach, rather than wasting time on methods better suited to fair-dealing in a spirit of good faith or equality.

Recognizing Your Priorities

It's important to keep your needs in mind when you enter a conflict, but it's just as important not to be blinded by them. You want to allow room for the other person's needs, for instance. And you want to be able to see your needs in perspective; to recognize your priorities. You need to consider how important your goal is, relative to the opposition you must overcome to achieve it. If your goal is worth it, it may be appropriate to take a more forceful stand to achieve it in that situation. Or you might find a way to attain that goal by pulling out of the situation and thereby avoiding the conflict. On the other hand, you may have other priorities, such as keeping the peace in a relationship or keeping a job. Those desires suggest backing down or compromising as more viable and pragmatic approaches—at least for the time being.

One man at a workshop complained about being in a situation he hated at work. Gary worked as a programmer. He tended to be a quiet, introverted person, and he felt depressed by the aggressive politicking and jostling for power he saw around him at work. As he commented: "I'm just sick of seeing day in and day out people in competition. I see managers butting heads, co-workers butting heads. And I just hate it." In particular, he felt his manager was constantly beating him down by telling him what to do and when to do it. She seemed to ignore what he said when he tried to speak up.

Gary wanted to know what to do about it. Should he be assertive and use a more competitive approach to stand up to her? Give in and accommodate? Should he avoid the situation entirely, by looking for and finding another job? Or was some sort of compromise or collaboration possible? Since she had so much more power, he rather doubted that he had any options but to give in, as he was doing. But that left him feeling resentful.

To decide what to do, Gary had to begin by looking at his priorities. He had to consider what the probable outcomes were of using different styles to respond to the conflict. Accordingly, in the workshop, I asked him to list and rate his priorities. "What's most important to you? Keeping your job? Finding a new job? Standing up to your manager and getting your way, no matter the cost?"

With the workshop members, Gary looked at each of the possible options and the likely outcome of each. Since he had talked about a desire to stand up to his boss, the group considered the competitive approach first. Gary realized it wasn't worth it to combat his boss directly, because she had more power and was the type of person who liked to get her own way. Thus, a competitive approach probably wouldn't work. It would just put him in direct confrontation with his boss, and since she had more power, she would win. He might even lose his job.

What about the accommodation approach he was using now? It was keeping his boss happy and his job secure, at least. But it was also making him miserable. One way to deal with this was to use a personal avoidance technique in combination with accommodation. That let Gary insulate himself psychologically from the personal fall-out of a yielding approach. Specifically, Gary learned the following avoidance techniques to protect himself from his negative feelings about giving in to his boss:

- Do some visualizations or internal exercises to tell yourself: "I'm not going to let this bother me."
- Try putting up a protective wall of white energy around yourself by visualizing it or telling yourself it is there. Then, you can use this to deflect any negative feelings you experience from this negative person. You can just experience these negative feelings bouncing off this shield, while you stay centered and safe from attack.
- Remind yourself that if you are going to stay in this same place and continue to work there, you have to deal with a person you don't like. Just keep telling yourself that's one of the conditions that goes with the job and you can't let it get to you.

However, if Gary felt the situation was just too oppressive, this accommodation-avoidance approach might not work very well. In that case, it might be better to avoid the situation entirely by quitting or perhaps transferring to a new department, if possible.

Finally, Gary looked at the collaborative and compromise options. Neither seemed a productive possibility, because his boss had so much more power than he did. She hardly seemed open to giving up any of her power to respond to any of his needs. Since the collaborative and compromise approaches require relatively equal footing—so each can give some and take some—they rarely work in such unequal power situations.

After considering the various options, it looked like Gary's only real choices were accommodation and avoidance—if he wanted to keep his job. If that was too painful for him, he could leave. Since he did place a high priority on keeping the job, he rejected that last option. Accommodation hadn't been working well from his standpoint, although objectively it seemed the best option. To counteract his own feelings of resentment, and make this technique work, Gary decided he would try coupling it with internal avoidance techniques. If this didn't work out to his satisfaction, he might have no recourse but avoidance. Short of leaving the company, he might request a transfer to another department or a new supervisor. At least avoidance promised a final solution to the conflict.

Becoming Aware of Real Issues and Interests

Just as you must look past your surface desires in a conflict to consider your priorities, you must also look beneath these surface desires to assess both your own and the other party's deeper needs and interests. Your surface wants, demands, or positions are what may spark the conflict, because you both have wants, demands, or positions that seem to be incompatible. However, these wants, demands, or positions may just be symptoms of those deeper concerns that are of greatest importance to each of you. While it may not be possible to satisfy the seemingly important surface desires, there may be ways to resolve those truly important underlying needs or concerns.

Becoming aware of what you really need and really want is the key. If you're not sure what you want, you won't know how best to get it.

For this reason, a key factor in deciding how to work towards a solution is awareness. (Awareness will also help you recognize those situations where it's not even *worth* struggling towards a resolution.) Basically, the three types of awareness to have are

1) an awareness of your own surface wants and underlying interests;

2) an awareness of the other party's surface wants and underlying interests;

3) an awareness of what you and the other person may require to satisfy these wants or needs.

There are two ways to develop this awareness. One is to get the issues and interests out in the open and talk about them directly. The other is to use your sensitivity or intuition to look underneath the surface and try to fathom what is really going on for the person with whom you are in conflict.

The previous chapter discussed both methods in detail, as well as the necessity of getting to underlying interests to forge any kind of long-term, satisfying resolution in a situation where these deeper interests are really important. But in many everyday situations, for efficiency's sake, you may not want to take the time to deal with these. For example, you may not want to deal with your neighbor's underlying interest in putting his car in front of *your* house most of the time when you want that space. In that situation, you may choose an approach to conflict that focuses on surface issues—compromise, say—instead of one that has you look deeper—collaboration. To come to that decision, you'd have to be aware that underlying interests exist, but that they don't necessarily bear on a resolution. That way you wouldn't be thrown off course if your neighbor brings up political arguments (such as the right to park freely on the public streets). You can just work on what you can offer to get him to do what you want to create a compromise (such as not doing something he doesn't like: honking your horn to hurry up your kids to go to school in the morning).

On the other hand, you'll want to recognize those situations where you need to dig deeper and choose an appropriate style. Say if the other person seems very unhappy about what seems to you a trivial situation; consider that he or she might have deep-rooted, concealed interests there. Such an awareness might lead you to accommodate that person, and write your surface wants off as less important than that person's deeper needs. Or you might seek to collaborate if your needs seem equally important. In either collaboration or this accommodation from power (rather than the usual giving in from weakness), you'll try to get the other person to share his or her needs. One such technique to use in getting to underlying interests is active listening. You'll also want to get your *own* underlying needs and interests out in the open during collaboration. Visualization and self-awareness techniques will help you here. The point is be aware of the different levels of wants and needs that can exist; your ability to choose which to deal with; and the fact that the different approaches to conflict can help you address particular needs.

Being Aware of Your Options for Response

It may take some time to develop a full awareness of the different strategies and when best to apply them. But as you keep thinking about them and using them, in time this awareness will become a natural part of your life. You will have developed a better ability to respond in an appropriate way when you encounter any conflict or potential conflict. In fact, after a while, you will become so aware that your awareness will operate on a nearly unconscious level, like being on automatic pilot.

For example, suppose you are in an ongoing conflict situation with a neighbor or someone at work. It's a conflict situation that recurs on a daily or weekly basis, whenever you encounter this person. Initially, you might approach the conflict consciously thinking about what conflict handling approach to use. And perhaps you might sort through the different styles, thinking something like: "Well, this particular approach hasn't worked before, so what other approach might I try now?" This strategy of *consciously* thinking about your own situation in light of the description of each separate style is a good way to begin.

But soon you'll be able to choose easily—from experience—what style is most appropriate and most comfortable for you in each situation, whether it is standing up for your rights, walking away and avoiding the situation, or otherwise accommodating, compromising, or trying to find a resolution through collaboration. You'll create your own expertise and catalogue of effective (and not-so-effective) approaches.

Using a Series of Strategies To Deal With a Conflict

One appropriate conflict style may be all you need to resolve some conflict. But in other cases, you may need to use a combination of styles, particularly if it is a complex or ongoing conflict. Or you may find one style useful for resolving a part of the conflict, but then require a different style to deal with other parts of it. And one style may be fine for resolving the conflict for a time, but then, if the conflict resurfaces, you may need to use another style to contain or diffuse it again.

For example, suppose a conflict with co-workers erupts at a time when you are under a great deal of pressure. You don't want to try to resolve the situation at that moment. So you might start off with a style of avoidance to delay dealing with the issue. But then you discover that one of the people is under deadline pressure and needs your immediate help to sort things out. It might be that this demand for help, without anything offered in return or any regard for your own situation, makes you resentful. It might even exacerbate the conflict. However, given the deadline, you might feel it appropriate to accommodate the person temporarily to get through the deadline. Then, with the time pressure over, you can sit down and air your concerns. That might be a good time to work towards some mutually agreeable solution through compromise or collaboration.

As you pay more attention to working through conflicts, you will find you become more sensitive to the appropriate approach to use. You'll also find it helps to stay flexible, so you can shift strategies if your first attempt isn't working.

Also, in some situations you may use any number of styles to deal with different aspects of the conflict. For instance, you might compromise to get some points out of the way, accommodate to the other person's greater needs in another area, press competitively for what you really want on some issue, avoid dealing with other topics entirely if you decide they really aren't that important, and use collaboration for some of the most deeply felt concerns both you and the other person have. An involved negotiation over a long-term business deal or a personal relationship might be a good example of how these varying styles might come into play over time.

The best way to sharpen your own skills in using and choosing among the styles is real life practice. However, the exercises below can help to prepare you for these real life conflicts by giving you a chance to preplan what you might do so you feel more confident and assured when the time comes.

Exercise #1: Visualization

By playing out a conflict or an encounter in your mind ahead of time, you can anticipate the results of various approaches. This will help you pick out the style most likely to succeed, while you still have a chance to use it. It may also give you the distance and objectivity you need to gain insights into the motivations and fears of different parties in the conflict. The following visualization exercise will help you try out different approaches. Read the script below into a tape recorder, if you can. (Or alternatively, just keep the general guidelines in mind and create your own visualization.) Before you record it, read through it and make a few changes to tailor it to your situation. Once you've recorded it in a soothing authoritative voice, close your eyes, take three deep breaths, and concentrate.

I'd like you to start off by getting relaxed. Focus on your breathing. Feel your chest and stomach expand with each breath, and then release. Just close your eyes and pay attention, as you let your breathing go in, and out; in, and out; in, and out. And as you get relaxed, you are going to stay alert and awake, and you're going to be able to pay attention to the sound of my voice.

Now, imagine a screen in a theater. You're in the theater looking at the screen, and there's some problem situation that comes to mind. You might see yourself on the screen, and maybe you see other people, too.

It might be a situation at work. It might be a situation involving a friend or family member. It might be an internal situation.

It could be something you have to make a decision about now. Or maybe it's something you could put off for a week, two weeks, or more. It might be a conflict situation that just happened, or it might be an ongoing situation.

Whatever the conflict situation is, you're seeing it on the screen, and you're watching it play itself out. You feel a certain distance from it, because you are sitting in the audience watching. And even though you may be a character in the scene, you're also removed from it, because you are watching.

And now, as you watch, imagine the different approaches you might use to resolve the conflict. Maybe you have a particular objective, and it's very important to you. So you might want to take an assertive style, a more competitive kind of style to do what you want to get the situation resolved in your way. If so, notice what you say; notice how others react. And notice how others feel.

Or perhaps you are seeing something that's not that important to you. You're willing to give in and let go of it. If so, you might want to adopt a more accommodative style. If you do, notice what that feels like.

Or maybe this is the kind of conflict you feel you want to avoid. You'd like to put it away or walk away from it, if you can. In this case, you might choose the avoidance style. If so, you might leave, and you can think about what would happen if you walked away. Or, if you can't actually leave physically, you can visualize yourself having a protective screen of white light around you. This protective screen keeps the conflict away from you, so you don't have to think about it or pay attention to it. Yet, at any time you can drop the protective screen and deal with the conflict situation in other ways. So notice how this approach feels to you and how it works.

Or, if this is a conflict that is important and worth resolving carefully, you want to take the time and effort to work things out. If so, perhaps there is one person you need to talk to, to work out this resolution. Now, if you want, you can picture yourself talking to this person, working together, collaborating to achieve this resolution.

Or it may be that you are experiencing a conflict going back and forth in your own mind. You want to take the time to deal with this and work out a resolution. So now imagine two parts of yourself sitting down and talking about the conflict, one side with one point of view, and the other with its opposite. As they talk, each side expresses its needs and attempts to find common interests.

Finally, this might be a situation where you can give a little and the other person can give a little towards a compromise. Or if it's an internal conflict, part of you can give a little and another part of you can give a little. So maybe a compromise might work. If so, picture what this compromise might look like.

Now, having reviewed the possible conflict styles you can choose, recall which felt the most right, for you can choose among any of those styles. And see it play on the screen.

Now watch yourself making some kind of decision and choosing a particular style. Or perhaps imagine yourself choosing a series of styles, to deal with the problem now. Or if you don't want to look at the problem now, you can always use avoidance for now, and deal with the problem later.

If any questions or problems come up in using any particular style, they will come to mind now. You may have other questions you must resolve first, in order to resolve your conflict. Let any of these questions or problems come to mind now, and notice what you need to do to resolve them.

Now, whatever style you have chosen, I'd like you to see the problem resolved. You see your ideal solution occurring before you. You see your goal, and you experience a feeling of peace and harmony.

So now you're feeling very good and very comfortable with that solution. And you know you can always use that approach again when other conflicts come up. You can always go to the theater and see the conflict on the screen in front of you. You can always choose among these different styles, watch each possibility played out, and then see the conflict resolved.

And now, feeling very good, seeing this resolution, I'd like you to let the issue go. See this conflict on the screen or the resolution you have achieved slowly dissipate. Watch it fade away.

And now notice the credit on the screen. You can thank yourself, because your name is up there as the director. You are totally in charge of this conflict, in resolving it. And you're there as the scriptwriter. And you're there as the starring actor.

And you feel very, very good about having this control. And you feel very good about the creativity you've shown in resolving the conflict.

Now the credits are finished. You start getting up from the movie theater, and as you walk out into the light, I'm going to start counting backwards from five to one. As I do, you're going to become more and more awake and come back into the room. Five, four, more and more awake. Three, back into the room. Two, one. And when you are ready, open your eyes and come back.

Exercise #2: Mapping Out Possibilities

Sometimes it helps to write down or map out all the possible approaches to a conflict without going through the ritual of visualization. To do this, begin by clarifying the problem. Ask yourself if yours is a one-time type of conflict, or whether it reflects a recurring pattern. The latter requires a more general and comprehensive kind of response. Once the issue is clearer in your mind, you can look at how you might apply each of the approaches you are considering to the problem. This includes considering the various ways in which the other party might respond to each method. With the aid of the chart at the end of this chapter, you can rate your estimate of the probabilities of each response, and note how much you would like each particular outcome. When you multiply your probability estimate by your style preference score, you'll see a list of numerical scores, and can easily select the best approach to use.

For example, at a workshop, one man imagined the possible approaches and results in dealing with a conflict situation involving a close friend. What disturbed him was that after a long, close friendship the two of them appeared to be drifting apart. Jim wasn't sure whether to discuss the problem with the friend, try to reestablish closer ties in other ways, or just let the relationship drift away. As he described the problem: "I'm really not certain what to do. I feel Bob has become very self-centered and doesn't show much interest in the relationship. But in the past, we were such good friends. We've shared a lot together. I'd hate to lose that."

Jim wasn't sure what to do. However, before he could start thinking about the possibilities, he needed to clarify the problem. Was this an isolated problem involving this particular person, or was this a pattern he experienced with other people? If an isolated problem, then Jim should consider a more targeted response to deal with this particular situation. However, if he noticed a series of similar conflicts in his life, this might suggest a need for making broader changes, perhaps in himself and his general approach to friendships.

After some thought, Jim concluded this was a particularized situation, involving just his relationship with Bob and not his relationships in general. His next step was to focus on what he could or wanted to do about that. For Jim, a key concern was that he had let the relationship drift along in this unsatisfying way for so long that he felt funny about even raising the subject with Bob. On the other hand, he felt if he didn't say anything, the two of them might just continue to drift apart. He knew he didn't want that.

It was time for Jim to examine his alternatives and the likely outcomes of each approach. The workshop members helped Jim think about the different approaches he might consider and the results: their advice is printed below. To go through this process yourself, list the various alternatives to your own problem and think about the likely results of each. Then, you can proceed with rating these alternatives: use a five-point scale, with 1 for extremely undesirable and 5 for most desirable (3 is average or neutral). The following discussion with Jim is designed to illustrate how the process might work. This is what he was told:

> From what you are saying, you have several possibilities. First, you can say nothing, which is one form of accommodating or giving in to the situation as it exists now. In that case, it sounds like the relationship will continue to drift apart, leading to the end of the relationship.

Secondly, if you feel dissatisfied, you could just end the relationship yourself, rather than letting it drift. That's a way of avoiding the situation by cutting it off yourself.

Thirdly, if you do say something, you might be able to repair the relationship by bringing it back to where it used to be, if you are able to raise the subject in a comfortable way and your friend proves receptive. Then, depending on how extensive your discussion is, this would be a form of compromise or collaboration. To try this, it might be worth saying to your friend something like: "Well, there's something that has been bothering me for a while, and I'd like to talk about it with you, if you'd like to listen." There is always the chance, of course, that your friend might not want to talk about it or won't prove receptive, so attempting a discussion could lead to the end of the relationship, too, particularly if directly confronting the issue does upset your friend. But on the other hand, the discussion does offer the possibility of saving the relationship if you bring up these issues, whereas all of the other alternatives would seem to suggest the relationship will end.

Finally, since the competitive style is not appropriate here—you obviously can't force a mutual friendship on someone, there's no need to think about that.

Thus, in assessing these possibilities, you need to ask yourself how valuable the relationship is to you, and you can use the chart to help you decide. If you feel like you'd like to try to get it back to the way it was, it may be worth trying for a discussion with your friend. For if you feel it has value to you, maybe you can make one last stab to see if you can work out the problem, and if not, just let it go.

Finally, if you do let it go, allow yourself to feel okay about doing that by realizing that relationships can develop to a certain point, and they can be very good and valuable ones. But then you may go in one direction, and the other person can go in another, so that it becomes appropriate to let the relationship go, because you have developed different concerns.

An example of Jim's use of the chart is illustrated on the following page. It helped him decide that it was worth it to have an open discussion about their relationship with his friend in the hopes of saving it. Similarly, you can use the chart (you can make copies of the one on the page after that) to help you come up with your own alternatives to the conflicts you face. If you are honest and thoughtful in rating the options, the chart should help you settle on your best choices.

Once you have selected an alternative, you may still need to think about the best way to make it work. Jim, for example, decided he did want to make one last attempt to restore his close friendship with Bob. Since the chart indicated he valued the friendship enough to give it one last try, and he felt the more in-depth collaborative approach would offer the hope of creating a more deeply satisfying relationship if it worked. However, he wasn't sure of the best way to raise the topic so his friend would be receptive. Thus, he decided to talk it out ahead of time. In some cases, it's helpful to get input or suggestions from others, and that's what Jim sought out. You might also spend some time imagining what you'll say or do in advance, so you are optimally prepared before you actually do it. The following example is the advice I gave Jim. It will help you see how you might map out your own strategy in advance.

If you feel this is a sensitive subject to discuss, you might start by letting your friend know that you have had certain things come up for you and you would like to discuss them if your friend is willing. If not, that's the end of that possibility. But if your friend is receptive, maybe you can sit down for coffee or go out for dinner together. The idea is to find a supportive, comfortable setting.

When you raise the topic, you can do it casually. Show that you want to be supportive and helpful, and try to be as diplomatic as possible. You might say something like: "This has been of concern to me, and maybe you have some concerns about it, and so I'd like to hear what you have to say about it." Before you explain your point of view, you might preface it by saying how much you value your friendship and how you feel like you've done a lot together. Your friend should feel your care and concern.

After preparing the way, you can move on to the more sensitive subject. You might ask if perhaps something has been happening in your friend's life to distract him from the friendship and your attempts to connect better. Listen to his answer before you raise any of the other concerns that have been bothering you.

The point is that you want to put this discussion in the context of saying that you really value the person's friendship and want to stay friendly. You also want to correct something that has been bothering you to make things better. In saying these things, you should emphasize how you feel and what you perceive. Avoid sounding like you are accusing the person. Also, recognize that your friend may have a different perspective on what has happened, and make it clear that you want to understand it. Let him know that you really want to work things out.

If your friend feels he wants to talk about it, fine. You will be well on your way to working out a resolution. But if he doesn't or feels threatened by this discussion, then you can let the relationship go, knowing that at least you tried to do what you could.

The last two chapters have suggested various ways in which you can think about dealing with conflicts in everyday life. They are designed to help you retain control and flexibility by choosing among different conflict styles and applying them as appropriate. As you become familiar with these styles and learn to use them on a regular basis, you will find that you can use them automatically in response to many conflict situations. You will come to know which one to use, as if by second nature.

In dealing with more serious, complex, or ongoing conflicts, such as those described in this chapter, you may want to use more specialized conflict techniques: visualization or mapping out the possibilities. With time, these too will come easily to you.

Mapping Out Possibilities

Description of the Conflict: _____ I feel a formerly good relationship is breaking up and I'd like to keep this relationship if possible

Is this a one-time conflict? ___✓___

a recurring conflict? _____

Rating Scale: 1 = least probable/desirable
3 = average probability/neutral desirability
5 = most probable/desirable

Possible Approaches (describe in detail)	Possible Responses of the Other Party or Probable Result of Using that Style	Probability of Response (1-5)	Desirability of Outcome (1-5)	Score (Probability x Desirability)
Avoidance: ending the relationship now	immediate end of the relationship	5	1	5
Accommodation: letting things drift as is	gradual end of the relationship	3	2	6
Competition: not applicable	–	–	–	–
Compromise: talking about how we have some good times in the past and how it would be nice to continue the friendship	relationship will end anyway or relationship will be patched up and continue	3 3	2 3	6 9
Collaboration: exploring in-depth advantages of the relationship and how it could be mutually satisfying	relationship will end anyway or relationship will be patched up and continue	3 3	2 4	6 12

Mapping Out Possibilities

Description of the Conflict: _____

Is this a one-time conflict? _____

a recurring conflict? _____

Rating Scale: 1 = least probable/desirable
3 = average probability/neutral desirability
5 = most probable/desirable

Possible Approaches (describe in detail)	Possible Responses of the Other Party or Probable Result of Using that Style	Probability of Response (1-5)	Desirability of Outcome (1-5)	Score (Probability x Desirability)
Avoidance:				
Accommodation:				
Competition:				
Compromise:				
Collaboration:				

9

Negotiating Win-Win Solutions

Once you decide a conflict is worth resolving without avoiding the matter, giving in to what someone else wants, or forcing through your own resolution because you have the power to do so, you are left with a problem to work out through negotiation. You have to find the common ground between your desired solution and the other party's.

The two ways of negotiating this are through compromise or collaboration. The two approaches are similar in involving some give and take and back and forth. Each works towards a solution that gives everybody some of what he or she wants. The major difference is that compromise focuses on surface issues and wants, and collaboration strives to go deeper.

In compromise, both parties outline their positions at the outset, or at least what they think they want. Then, each party begins making concessions and considering counteroffers, until an agreement is reached somewhere in the center. This is a common approach to settling money matters: haggling over a price, or negotiating a fair salary.

By contrast, in collaboration, you go beyond the initial positions to look at the underlying interests, needs, and concerns of the parties. It can take some time and some digging for these to come to light. But the effort to explore these issues is part of the collaborative process, since a satisfactory solution takes all these factors into consideration. It resolves each party's concerns more thoroughly than a compromise. Collaboration takes more time and energy than most other conflict handling styles, but it often offers the best chance for forging a win-win solution.

Chapter 7 presents a more in-depth discussion and comparison of the two styles, as well as descriptions of the three other major conflict-handling styles. You may wish to refer back to that chapter if the terms aren't familiar to you.

You might know that you want to work towards a win-win solution. But how do you know which method—compromise or collaboration—would be most appropriate? As with choosing any approach to conflict resolution, the key lies in being aware of the specific circumstances surrounding a conflict, and in remaining aware and flexible as negotiations proceed. Generally, the circumstances for most appropriately using the two methods differ enough to make most choices clear. The tips below should help you distinguish between those situations where compromise is especially useful and those where collaboration may be best.

Choose compromise when:

- the issues are relatively simple and clear-cut
- there isn't much time to reach a solution or you want to achieve a resolution as quickly as possible
- it would be better to achieve a temporary agreement quickly, and then deal with the more serious or underlying issues later
- you and the other party (or parties) to the negotiation aren't that concerned about the goals or outcome of conflict
- you haven't been able to resolve the matter using collaboration or you haven't been able to get your way by using your own power to force a solution

Choose collaboration when:

- the issues are fairly complex and require a detailed discussion to work out a solution acceptable to both
- both parties are willing to spend the time needed to deal with the underlying needs and concerns
- both parties feel their concerns are very important and don't want to compromise on them
- both parties are willing to be open-minded and approach the negotiation in a spirit of good faith, which includes being willing to listen and understand the other's concerns

- both parties want to achieve a permanent agreement, rather than a quick temporary solution, and are willing to deal with the issue now

Why Win-Win Solutions Are Possible

Most conflicts stem from numerous sources and reasons, and that one fact makes win-win solutions possible. Initially, it may seem like a conflict is rooted in two unreconcilable positions. Both parties can even be emotionally invested in the opposing positions they have taken. But almost always, the parties have more than one reason for entering the conflict, because of their various underlying interests or needs. Moreover, the parties normally attach different priorities to these reasons, and there are usually several possible positions that could satisfy a particular need. The key to resolving a conflict the win-win way is to recognize and satisfy as best as possible each person's highest priorities or most important needs in return for getting concessions on lower priority items or needs.

Experts in negotiation know this. When called in to help settle disputes, they look for these underlying reasons, interests, or needs. Once these are identified, mediators encourage one party to give in on areas of lower priority in return for getting concessions from the other to satisfy higher priority desires. Or they try to find new alternative positions that provide good payoffs for both. Such exchanges of concessions or new creative possibilities can be the key to a win-win solution.

This kind of approach is used by Fred E. Jandt, the author of *Win-Win Negotiating*, who leads conflict management seminars for professionals in business and public service groups. As he observes: "One of the most effective techniques in conflict management is to identify all the sources of a particular conflict and to persuade the parties to compromise some in order to obtain concessions on others." And the reason he uses this approach is because "There is never *only one* source of conflict. There may be one source to which both parties attach more importance than any other, and that source may or may not be the precipitating factor when the conflict flares up. However, inevitably, inescapably, and invariably, there will always be at least one secondary source."

Step 1. Get Emotions Under Control

It can take some time to identify these underlying sources and multiple interests to a conflict. And it can seem difficult and confusing at first to try to do so. But give yourself some time to practice and develop this awareness of issues beneath the surface. Realize that it is this variety of sources and reasons that provides you with multiple possibilities for resolving a conflict so that everybody wins.

If you are involved in a conflict where negotiation seems appropriate, the key is to look beneath the surface of the expressed positions: both the other party's (or parties') and your own. Before you can do that, everybody has to get his or her emotions under control so you can reasonably and rationally explore these underlying interests, concerns, reasons, and needs.

To help you achieve these win-win solutions, the practical steps are outlined below.

If emotions are high on either side, take it upon yourself to begin work on clearing the air. It might not be possible to resolve all those feelings of anger, hurt, or resentment at once, but it is crucial that they at least be diffused or set aside for the moment. Only then can you both deal calmly with the problem. Your job is to get your own emotions under control, and to appeal to the other party to do the same.

For example, you might say something like: "Look, I know you're angry. I've been feeling much that way myself. But if we're going to resolve this, we have to put our feelings aside and try to work on some alternatives. Would you be willing to do that?"

If the person still isn't ready to put feelings aside, you might say something like: "I know you're still very angry and I'd like to understand why you feel that way. Maybe we can talk briefly about the misunderstandings that caused this problem. And *then* maybe we can talk about what we can do about it."

You want to let the person know that you do want to spend some time dealing with the problem, and that you are willing to put any emotions aside so you can do this. This doesn't mean denying all those feelings; rather, what you are trying to do is acknowledge those feeling and put them in perspective so they don't interfere with achieving a resolution. A good way to do this is to allow each of you a little time to vent briefly about how you feel. But then suggest you might both try to go on, and that achieving a resolution might itself help to get rid of any remaining anger or resentment. If it doesn't and the person still feels it necessary, you can stop and take the time to share and address those feelings again. But now, make clear your hope that you can both move on. If the other person has calmed down in response to your own calmness and recognizes the logic of your position, you'll be able to do so. In short, your focus should be on releasing the emotions and moving on; not getting stuck in going over and over the feelings and the reasons for them.

If these initial efforts to diffuse emotions don't work, or seem inappropriate in light of the emotional intensity surrounding the conflict, you may need to do some more work on these emotions before you can go on. Refer back to Part 1 for a more detailed discussion on dealing with emotional issues. You should see this process not as a mere prelude to negotiations, but as an integral part of the resolution process.

Step 2. Agree on Ground Rules

It is useful to set up some ground rules in the beginning negotiation phase, especially if emotions have been high or if you are trying to resolve things with someone who is unfamiliar with the negotiation process. Take the lead here, if you can. Explain that these rules are designed to keep the process going smoothly.

Some of the basic rules to suggest include:

- Agreeing to listen to each other as carefully as you can
- Agreeing not to interrupt each other
- Agreeing not to get angry or express hostility even if one disagrees with something being said
- Agreeing to treat each other with respect
- Agreeing on the amount of time you want to devote to the process
- Agreeing to try to see the other's point of view

Such rules are set forth by mediators and local conflict resolution groups at the beginnings of their negotiation sessions to help the parties talk about their disputes and resolve them. The rules set a tone of mutual respect and fair play, and help set the stage for productive negotiation. Similar rules can achieve the same effect for you.

Once you've laid out ground rules, you can always refer to them later if the negotiation process breaks down or tempers start rising. Such a breakdown in the process is a signal to call time out, and refocus everyone back on the goal of the negotiation to keep things on track. You might say something like: "Listen, I know you're feeling really angry. But we agreed we would try to listen to each other and treat each other with respect. If you can just let me finish what I was trying to say, then I'd like to listen to you."

For maximum effectiveness, be sure to get the other person's agreement when you set the rules, as well as his or her suggestions for additional rules. Usually it will be easy to agree here, since you are merely suggesting rules of ordinary human courtesy and respect. If you can't seem to agree, take that as a sign that the feelings underlying the conflict may still run too deep. Or perhaps this may be an indicator that the other party is not coming from a place of good will. That is a barrier to a successful outcome, because both parties need to approach a negotiation in a spirit of good faith for a mutually satisfying result. If you think this is the case, consider alternative approaches to resolution: avoidance, accommodation, or simply forcing your way through. But if you still think there are hopes for negotiation, return to Step 1.

Step 3. Clarify Positions

Once the emotional thicket is trimmed down, and rules are set, think of the first phase of negotiation as a chance to get all the issues, opinions, positions, and views out in the open. If the other person is equally attuned to getting everything out on the table, you can expect to express your own concerns, too. But first, you want to find out where the other person is coming from; what he or she perceives, wants, and needs. This will help you shape your own proposals, taking that person's desires and concerns into consideration. You'll still be seeking to gain what you most want. But you'll help the other person feel heard and understood, and in doing so improve *your* chances of being received in a positive way.

Here are some guidelines for understanding the other's position.

- *Look at the world from the other's point of view.* Try to step into the other's shoes for a while, so you can imagine what that person is thinking or perceiving. This can help you in assessing what he or she thinks is important, what he or she is willing or not willing to give up what he or she fears, and so forth. You don't have to agree with this point of view, but you need to understand it. The empathy will improve your rapport as you negotiate, and it will even help you in influencing the other person to accept an agreement. After all, if you seem to understand where he or she is coming from, he or she will trust you more.
- *Avoid making judgments about what the other person thinks, believes, or has done.* Sure, you may think you are right. The other person probably thinks he or she is right, too. Even if the other person is clearly wrong, he or she may not want to admit it to you (or to him- or herself). As a general rule, it is not helpful to start criticizing or blaming the other person, even if the other person did make a mistake. It will just make the other person defensive and resistant to you or your ideas. That person may start criticizing or blaming *you* to feel better or to even the score, and negotiations are likely to give way to heated exchanges and hurt feelings.

  What do you do if the other party starts blaming or criticizing you? Try not to jump at the bait and attack or get defensive in kind. Just keep in mind your goal of seeking to negotiate some resolution for the future, and try to move as quickly as possible to that. If you can, refer back to the rule you set about not expressing hostility.
- *Discuss any differences in perceptions, assumptions, and beliefs.* Differences in outlook and interpretation can be a major block to negotiating an agreement, so you want to get them out in the open to correct them. If, for example, someone assumes you agreed to do something you never did, that

might lead the person to think you are irresponsible and to distrust your attempts to guide the negotiation process. So, to alter that person's impression, you have to make it clear what really happened (i.e.: you never agreed). Do so in a way that allows the other person to accept that he or she has an incorrect perception. You don't want to accuse or blame the other person for being wrong. Rather, it is better to point out that you both may have different perceptions, assumptions, or beliefs, and that you want to clear up any confusions. Sometimes just bringing these perceptions, assumptions, and beliefs out in the open is enough to clarify matters. You can bridge the gaps in perception.

Discussing any differences in understanding in this open, non-threatening way makes it easier for either of you to acknowledge being mistaken, if you are. Should it become clear that you are correct about something, but the other person has difficulty recognizing that he or she is mistaken, you may have to do a little bit more to support your view. One good way is to offer to provide proof of your assertions, if you can (such as letters, documents, a third party to corroborate your story).

If you have the time, demonstrate through your actions that certain perceptions are faulty. So act responsibly, or friendly, or be diligent, or whatever the other person accuses you of *not* being (but when you do, be sure to be honest; if you fake anything, it will be obvious). You might also write a warm letter of apology or send a gift or flowers to show you regret any misunderstandings or misperceptions the person may have had about you.

- *Involve the other person in the negotiation process even though you may be taking the lead.* It is important to let the other party feel he or she has contributed valuable ideas. That way, he or she has some stake in the resolution. During the negotiation process, you should encourage the other person to contribute suggestions on ways of working out the problem. If you can, frame your ideas so that they tie in with something the other person has said or with what you perceive to be the other person's way of thinking. And if, somehow, the other person proposes just what you want or even have already said, by all means let the person think it's his or her own great idea. People are generally more willing to carry out ideas they see as their own, and then you get what you want, too. That's the essence of a true win-win solution.

- *Keep your initial bargaining position reasonable and realistic.* Sometimes there is a tendency to start off with an extreme position, based on the notion that you'll each come down a little and meet somewhere in the middle. In traditional negotiations, starting off with a higher position can commonly result in a better outcome for you than if you start off low. But if you go too high, you can appear to be unreasonable and lead the other person into responding in kind with a position taking the opposite extreme. You thus begin very far apart. While you may think this approach will lead you both to end up with some neutral compromise in the middle, in fact, this distance can interfere with a cooperative spirit.

Starting off with distant, extreme positions can create a seige mentality for negotiation, where you are both adversaries, each trying to get the best of the other. By contrast, if you begin with a more reasonable and realistic position, it invites the other person to participate with you as a partner in your search for a resolution. This sets a tone of fairness, and makes it easier to achieve a resolution that works for you both.

And what if you do begin reasonably, and the other person takes advantage by coming on strong? Remain firm, and point out that you want to find a solution that is fair to you both. Emphasize the reasonableness of your offer, and explain your hope that the other person is willing to proceed in a spirit of fairness. It's a strong appeal, since people tend to have a sense of justice, and commonly the other person will come around.

Step 4. Explore Underlying Needs and Interests

Now, with emotional blocks cleared out of the way, the ground rules stated, and the basic issues on the table, you are ready to focus on a crucial step of win-win negotiation—getting and giving information on what you each really want and need out of this negotiation. That means going beyond initially stated positions to explore underlying feelings and reasons for wanting what you want. Here are some ways to proceed:

- *Ask Why the Other Chose That Position*
You want to know why a person has done something or says he wants something. You want to know what he needs, would like, expects, hopes for, is afraid of, or is concerned about in taking the particular position he has. By responding to those underlying needs, wants, expectations, hopes, fears, or concerns, you might be able to alter that person's position by coming up with some alternative method of achieving his goals.

As an example, imagine that the company you work for has a strict policy about workers coming to work at a certain time and leaving at a certain time. You are working on a special project and feel you could do a better job by working at home. When you suggest it, your boss says, "No, company policy." But then, if you start probing, you may find the reasons for this policy are that the company is afraid of people taking advantage of more flexible rules by not working as hard and by taking long breaks. Also, the company wants people on board so that when clients call, the employees will be there. Knowing those underlying reasons allows you to propose alternate choices that will really satisfy your boss (such as using time sheets at home to show time worked, offering to work extra hours for the commuting time saved, proposing a limited trial of a few days to show how much extra work you can do, etc). You have a better chance of getting your way while continuing to satisfy the other party, because you've helped to find a win-win solution for you both.

When you do ask these why questions, be sure to ask them in a neutral, concerned way, so the person feels you really want to understand where he is coming from. You want to avoid sounding like a cross-examiner asking the person to explain or justify his position. That would only make the person defensive and even resentful that you sound so righteous.

- *Ask Why Your Position Was Not Chosen*
Another way to probe for underlying needs and concerns is to find out why a person hasn't made the choice you consider

most reasonable and desirable. Again, frame your question in a neutral way, so it doesn't sound like you are accusing the person. Instead of saying "Why didn't you do that," ask "What were your reasons for choosing not to do ... ? I'd really like to understand how you felt about this." You are asking the same thing, but your approach is more friendly and comfortable. It lets the person feel safe in answering on a topic where you may disagree, and not like you are challenging him to defend his answer.

Listen carefully to the answer you receive. You might catch sight of the blocks standing in the way of action or resolution. Perhaps you can find ways to change the person's mind by helping to remove those blocks. Or perhaps those reasons will make sense to you, suggesting that you may not be able to seek change in this area. So it might make more sense to try for a change in the person's position somewhere else—or it might even make sense to consider that person's preferred resolution.

For example, suppose you and a friend are in a conflict over an issue of responsibility. Your friend promised to do something while you were away, but then didn't. It turns out that he didn't just forget, but he decided he didn't *want* to do these things. He also didn't tell you anything, leaving you to find out what hadn't happened. Without accusing your friend of irresponsibility, you might try to find out why he decided not to act. Once you have established this safe space and expressed real curiosity, your friend might feel comfortable telling you the real reasons. Maybe he felt you were asking too much: he felt obligated to agree to do you a favor, as a friend, but then he resented the pressure to say yes. So he just didn't do what he agreed to do, saying no with his actions. Once these real feeling are out in the open, you can deal with the expectations and limits of your friendship, not whether your friend did or didn't do some task.

Getting to that point requires careful questioning, careful listening, and a willingness to be open and honest yourself.

- *Probe for Multiple Interests*
Normally, both you and the other party will have more than one reason for holding a particular position. If there is more than one party on the other side, different individuals will contribute to the variety of motivating reasons, too. You'll want to get all

of these reasons out in the open. You'll probably want to share your multiple reasons, as well.

You can use the same methods of neutral questioning and active listening as described above to ferret out the various underlying reasons. Your concern for the other party should set the stage for a calm exchange of ideas, so you can air your own concerns, too. The key is to show you are aware that various causes are likely to exist for an action or a position. When you uncover one plausible idea, this may not be the only one, so don't stop. Acknowledge it, and then ask if there's anything else. If the other person seems uncertain, suggest possible additional issues or concerns yourself to encourage the other person to dig deeper, or further. Perhaps point out that you are aware that sometimes people have multiple interests, and you do yourself, so it would be helpful if you share them. That way you can see if there are areas of mutual agreement or complementary concerns, so you can both be in a better position to gain from negotiation.

Once you know all these reasons, and show you acknowledge and understand them, you can try to find out which ones are most important to the other person. By discovering this information about relative priorities, you have a basis for proposing some tradeoffs. You can compare the other party's priorities to yours, and try to find a way to get each of your most important needs met, while making concessions on the others.

If you find it confusing to keep all the multiple needs straight, particularly in a complex group conflict situation, it helps to make a list and write down who wants what. You might even do this as you discuss these concerns. Then, if it's not already clear, go over this list and note priorities. Circle the most important needs. If you need to, underline the second most important needs. As you rank and tag these important needs, the points on which you can negotiate should become clearer.

- *Talk About Your Own Interests and Needs*
  Satisfying your own needs as well as others' is important. So make your needs known, too. It helps to make them specific and concrete, even vivid in your descriptions, so the other side can really see and empathize with your problem. For instance, if you are having a dispute with an employer over a long put-off raise,

you might give some compelling reasons why your salary now feels inadequate. Of course, you'll want to have your employer's agreement to listen, and to have shown some concern about meeting his needs (i.e., how this raise will benefit him by making you a more motivated, committed worker). But then, if this is a situation where it is appropriate to express your own needs, you can describe them. As an example of how to be specific, you might describe how you have been expecting this promised raise so you can pay back a loan to support your ailing parents. Or how you have been planning to enroll in that evening master's degree program, which is currently just out of reach. Such specifics are better than just talking generally about the costs of inflation. And such vivid detail makes your needs come to life for the listener.

When you do talk about your own interests, be sure to show how you recognize the other side's needs and concerns. Make it clear that you're not trying to invalidate them or make them seem unimportant in explaining your own. One way to do this is to preface a discussion of your own needs by summarizing your understanding of what the other party wants. In the scenario described above, you might say something like: "I realize that the company has had to be careful about its costs because of increased competition. In fact, I think I've helped improve efficiency with this in mind over the past couple of years." As you present arguments for why you deserve more money, give plenty of specific detail on what you've done and what you're worth. Again, you want to make your perspective as clear and compelling as possible. You also want to make your interests sound like they are in the other party's interest, too. If you can get your listener to sympathize and agree—through vivid detail—this can help in reaching an agreement you want.

It's often a good idea, too, to explain your reasons, interests, or needs first, before you state your position. That way, the other person is more receptive to listening, because you have provided a meaningful context or rationale. If you start with your position first, many times the other party may block it out or become defensive. He will see that your position directly opposes his own, and will want to guard against it or push it back, much like an opposing team in football. But if you begin with your reasons for feeling as you do or wanting what you want, this helps the other party to see things from your point of view and to be more receptive to what you are saying.

As another example, consider a husband-wife scenario. The wife has been staying home to take care of the young kids, while the husband works in a factory. Now, she wants to put her children in a day care facility and return to work. Yet she knows this will anger her husband. He may feel threatened by her independence and worry about the kids staying with strangers. If she tells him her desired position immediately, this might easily cause an uproar. She can predict the whole scene. She'll say what she wants; he'll say he doesn't like it; she'll repeat her position, maybe accuse him of being selfish; and the fight will be on. By contrast, if she eases into her point of view—perhaps talking about how nice it would be to have some more money and time to enjoy the things they like together; how helpful it would be for the kids to have some more contact with other children; how much she would like to do something to expand her own interests—this might help him hear and consider the reasonableness of her proposal. It also might give the husband the space and inclination to share his own needs in a productive, amicable way. Then an emotional argument will be less likely.

Thus generally sharing your reasoning before stating a position—and making that reasoning detailed and vivid—is a good way to open up the door to a solution that works for you both.

Using reasons, interests, and needs to explain your position can thus help you keep things calm, humanize you, show the reasonableness of your position, and help the other person see things from your point of view.

Step 5. Generate Alternatives

Once you have a clear idea of what both parties want—having shared your own interests and needs and listened to the other person's—you are ready to move to the next phase of the negotiation: coming up with alternatives to meet these needs. You can try brainstorming alternatives with the other party. Or you may have to do some brainstorming work on your own, and then present your best options to the other party later. You'll find more details on brainstorming to generate alternatives in the chapter on coming up with alternatives. But here are some basic considerations to keep in mind:

- *Suspend Judgment: Quantity Counts More Than Quality*
For now, you want to come up with as many possibilities as you can. Don't try to evaluate or critique them yet: this will inhibit the creative flow. Offer suggestions yourself, and invite suggestions from the other party or parties. Emphasize that you want to look at all the possible options now, and that you don't want to try to make any decisions about them until later. Tell people that even "crazy" or "impossible" ideas are welcome. Tell them that it doesn't matter who comes up with what ideas, since there's no judging and no person will be associated with any particular idea. Then everyone feels freer. Tell them that as ideas come up, you or someone else will write them down so everyone can see them.

Later, when you have a long list of ideas to choose from, you can go over all of them. That's when you'll decide which ones might be workable and look for combinations of workable ideas. You might think of the various options as trading cards with different values. You can choose which cards you want to put on the table, look at counteroffers—other people's cards—and eventually you will reach some agreement on which cards should be there. If you have trouble deciding which cards should be there, you might first decide which cards nobody wants at all. Then, eliminate unworkable possibilities by throwing those cards out. Afterwards, with the pool of options more manageable in size, you can better scrutinize and play with each card. Ultimately, you should narrow the pile down to the cards you both feel can create a win-win solution that works for everybody.

- *Focus on the Future*
Sometimes, even after you have dealt with emotions and talked about everybody's reasons and needs, there can be a temptation to express emotions and present explanations and justifications all over again. Resist this urge. It's important not to waste energy and poison a productive atmosphere by rehashing the past. If somebody begins to do this, gently interrupt. Indicate that you appreciate his or her feelings to provide some acknowledgement and reassurance. Then, remind him or her

that your focus should be on how to resolve the conflict for the future, not on what caused it in the past.

- *Remain Open to Different Alternatives*
  While it is helpful to have some sense of where you want to go in a negotiation, it's also critical to remain open to other ideas: both those you come up with and those the other person offers. The key is flexibility. You want to find some resolution that will satisfy your underlying needs or interests, as well as the other person's. Remember that there are many possibilities in each problem situation. Let yourself consider all the options, and avoid prematurely squelching or criticizing ideas you may consider wrong or crazy. Others may disagree, and these ideas just may work.

- *Avoid Closing Off Possibilities too Quickly*
  As you think about possible options, you may be tempted to reach a quick resolution and settle for the first reasonable alternative. And this can be fine if all parties feel really comfortable with this. But if you sense any doubts, or it feels like a resolution was reached too quickly for people to be comfortable with it, take the time to explore other options.

One reason for this tendency to jump at an early solution is that it can be hard to come up with options. Fisher and Ury, in their book *Getting to Yes*, explain: "Inventing options does not come naturally. *Not* inventing is the normal state of affairs. Moreover, they note that most people don't see inventing as part of the negotiating process. Rather, "people see their job as narrowing the gap between positions, not broadening the options available. They tend to think: " 'We're having a hard enough time agreeing as it is. The last thing we need is a bunch of different ideas.' " This thought follows from the desire for a single decision to result from the negotiation. It can feel like an expanded discussion of options and possibilities will only delay and confuse things.

The truth is that an open discussion of alternatives is what can uncover that really good solution that all parties feel comfortable with. It may take a little longer, but if the issue is really important or complex, it may be worth it. Remind yourself that many options exist; you may just have to work to see them. Try to convince others of this fact, and try to keep your discussion going until you feel that people have really stretched their imaginations to consider new possibilities. Occasionally, the first proposal may be so terrific that you all want to accept it instantly. If so, fine. But normally, it's a good idea to keep the channels open for a while.

Step 6. Agree on the Best Win-Win Options

As you propose solutions which have a payoff for you, describe the payoffs for the other person. This may help you to keep the discussions in the win-win spirit. The other person will see you care and be apt to respond in kind. At the same time, this approach will help you come up with win-win options in your proposals, and recognize the ones that don't hold win-win potential. After all, this is not a zero-sum, you-win/I-lose type of game. You aren't dealing with a limited universe, in which a gain for one person is a loss for the other. That might occur in a straight buyer-seller situation, where the more the seller charges, the more the buyer pays. But to resolve conflict, there can be gains on a number of levels, because people bring to a negotiation multiple interests and needs. Say an employee gives up salary benefits in return for a better position in the company; that could be seen as a gain both for the employee (in terms of status and pride) and the company (especially if it's seeing tight times and needs to cut back financially).

- *Help the Other Party Feel Comfortable Making Concessions or Giving Up Wants*

As you suggest possibilities or encourage the other person to think of alternatives, you may encounter resistance from that other person. If this occurs, it may be because he is beginning to see changes from an initial position as concessions or losses. Sometimes it's enough to emphasize that you're using negotiation as a process to find a mutually agreeable solution. But sometimes, if you feel these resistances occurring, you need to do more. One approach is to make it as comfortable as possible for the other person to let go of certain points. He should feel he is really gaining something in return for what he is giving up, or at least that his concessions will lead to a satisfying end result. Let the person save face and maintain a high self-image and self-esteem. It's a small concession for you to make for a bargaining move in your favor. Don't let the other party feel his image was slighted, in your eyes or his own.

One way to do this is to praise the person for any concessions. Let him know he's done something good or noble, and that he's making the whole process work. You want to acknowledge and support the person where you can and avoid any blaming or shaming. Thus, you don't want to accuse the person of being wrong or slow to admit responsibility for what he did; nor do you want to gloat when something seems to be turning your way. Rather, it's best to emphasize that you understand any difficulties he may be having in dealing with this difficult issue; that you really appreciate what the person is doing; and that things are going well for both of you.

This strategy saved the day at one conflict resolution panel. A teenage boy had borrowed a coat from a friend, and subsequently another tough boy in the neighborhood had taken the coat from him. The boy kept promising to get the coat back from the boy he knew took it, but he was not able to do so. The case finally ended up before a panel, because the coat's original owner really wanted it back, or at least for the other boy to reimburse him. For a long time, the boy who lost the coat kept hesitating, talking vaguely about his hopes of retrieving it. When it became apparent that he had no realistic chance of getting back the coat, he finally admitted—quite painfully— that yes, he was responsible, and with that he slumped in his seat like a deflated balloon. He had made a confession that was very difficult for him to make. But then, by praising him and supporting him for what he had done, the entire panel helped him feel better. He had given something up, it was true, but in return he got back his pride. And as a result, the two boys walked out of the session still friends.

Another way to help the person feel better about a concession is to build up what the person is getting in return. (For example, he may be giving up a room with a view, but his new office will be larger and more easily accessible to the office machines he regularly uses.)

Of course, you'll make the person feel much better if you can match the concession with one of your own. Think about this; even a minor point offered can reinforce the collaborative spirit. If you have nothing to offer, or it's inappropriate for you to concede anything more, be sure to express your appreciation. Point out that his concession is bringing both of you closer to a mutually satisfying solution.

Summing Up

In short, the overall model proposed in this book can be readily adapted for use in the negotiation process itself. You start by dealing with emotions to get them out of the way. Then, in a rational mode, you listen actively to the needs and reasons of the other person, showing that you've really heard them. Next, you share your own reasons and needs, describing them as vividly (and fairly) as you can. And finally, you move into the intuitive phase, where you throw out as many options as possible. You'll evaluate these later, choosing among them to come up with a resolution that provides some satisfaction for all parties involved. Your conflict will be resolved, and each party will feel a winner.

10

Learning To Deal
With Difficult People

The conflict resolution strategies described in this book are designed to work with most people under most everyday situations. But there are some people who won't respond to your best reasonable efforts at reconciliation. What can you do when you encounter an especially difficult person with certain personality characteristics that stand in the way of solving the problem or push your buttons and infuriate you?

There are some general principles you can turn to, incorporating principles already discussed in this book. In addition, you can use specific strategies to deal with some commonly identified categories of difficult people.

Who Are These Difficult People?

Each person may have his or her own category of difficult people, based on his or her own personality traits and past experiences. For example, a woman who has suffered for years as a child from an overprotective and possessive mother may find anyone who comes on as a stern, overbearing authority figure, particularly if female, a difficult person to deal with. Or a man who has divorced his nagging wife—a stickler for neatness—after a long courtroom battle may feel anyone who comes on as a perfectionist is someone who presents difficulties.

But apart from these special reasons for finding someone difficult, there are certain types identified as difficult by counselors, therapists, employers, researchers, and others who work or live with them. Descriptions of these people make the process of dealing with difficult people a little like bird watching: identify the personality type, and you know how to both categorize and deal with that person.

In a book that has become a classic, *Coping with Difficult People*, Robert M. Bramson identifies about a dozen different types, based on thirty years of experience in working with public and private organizations.[1] These include:

- The *hostile-aggressives*, divided up into the "sherman tanks," the "snipers," and the "exploders." These are the people who (respectively) try to bully others to get their way, make underhanded cutting remarks, or throw temper tantrums if no one listens.
- The *complainers*, who always have something to gripe about. They generally don't do anything to resolve the problem, though, because they feel powerless to do anything, or don't want to take the responsibility.
- The *clams*, who are silent and unresponsive. You don't know what they really think or want.
- the *super-agreeables*, who eagerly say yes to just about everything and appear to offer you support. They just don't follow through to produce what they say they will, or they act differently than they lead you to expect.
- The *naysayers* and *perennial pessimists,* who find a reason why anything suggested won't work. Since they usually think things will go wrong, they tend to say no most of the time or worry constantly after saying yes.
- The *know-it-all experts,* who act superior to everyone else because they think they know everything and want everyone else to know it. They may come across like "bulldozers," who push others out of the way with their knowledge. Or they may be more like "balloons," overinflated with their own knowledge and importance. It often turns out they are wrong, so they are just acting a part.

---

[1] Robert M. Bramson, *Coping with Difficult People,* New York: Ballantine Books, 1981, p. 4.

- The *indecisives* and *stallers*, people who have trouble making decisions because they are afraid of being wrong or not perfect. So they wait and wait, until the decision is made for them or until the need to make the decision is over.

Other difficult people include those who set up expectations, but then act contrary to them. Dr. George R. Bach, a psychotherapist, calls them "crazymakers," because they make people crazy by setting up the belief that a person or thing can be counted on to perform in a certain way, although the expected doesn't happen. As a result, their behavior breaks down the fundamental trust that must exist between people to smooth their interactions with each other.[2] Or perhaps you may encounter the other kind of crazymaker who sets up contradictory expectations and then expects you to meet them. Sometimes a crazymaker may ask you to do something, and then set up obstacles or otherwise sabotage your ability to achieve it, so you fail.

You can probably think of many other people with personality styles that make them difficult to deal with (possibly variations on some of these other types, or additional categories), such as:

- The *perfectionist*—the overrigid person who wants everything just so, even when it may not be necessary.
- The *secret fort*—the person who keeps everything in, won't tell you what's wrong, and then suddenly attacks you when you think everything is fine.
- The *innocent liar*—the person who covers his or her tracks with a lie or a series of lies, so you end up not knowing what to trust or believe.
- The *resentful altruist*—this is the person who appears to be helpful and giving, but then, under the surface, begrudges what he or she gives. You may feel this resentment percolating up in other encounters, or expressed non-verbally through unexpected sabotage or withdrawal.

---

[2] George R. Bach and Ronald M. Deutsch, *Stop! You're Driving Me Crazy*, New York: Berkley Books, 1979, pp. 5-6.

And then there are all the game players, such as the "yes, but-ers," described by Eric Berne in his book *The Games People Play*.[3] These are the people who act one way on the surface, without showing that they have some other hidden agenda. You don't know what's going on until you fall into their trap. It's a little like a bug flying in and out of a Venus Flytrap. At some point your wings will brush the edges of the game-playing person and the trap will close.

Your own list probably contains several more difficult types. But identifiying a type isn't enough. You need to know what to *do* when you must interact with someone on your list.

Some General Principles for Dealing With Difficult People

A good general principle to keep in mind in dealing with any kind of difficult person is that most people are difficult because they have certain underlying needs or interests that they meet by acting that way. The superaggressive person may act like a steamroller because underneath he is really afraid of dealing with people or having to confront the fear that he may be wrong; the silent clam may play it close to the vest because he is afraid of revealing himself to others; the perennial pessimist may always think things will go wrong because it is more comfortable to live with the certainty of failure than the uncertainty of hoping and finding those hopes unfulfilled. Thus, if you decide it's worth it to deal with people who are difficult, you might look for these underlying needs and think of how you can satisfy them. It's the same idea as taking an individual's needs into consideration in an everyday conflict situation.

In fact, you might run through the various principles and strategies outlined in this book and think about how they might apply to the particular situation you are in. Then, you can apply these, as well as the strategies which follow, for dealing with common types of difficult people.

---

[3] Eric Berne, *The Games People Play*, New York: Grove Press, 1964.

Working Through the Emotional Charges Triggered by a Difficult Person

Dealing with a difficult person can make you upset, angry, frustrated, depressed, or otherwise emotionally off-center. The difficult person him- or herself may be emotionally charged, like the exploder who throws a temper tantrum to get his or her way.

Thus, one of the first steps is getting your own emotions under control or helping the other person blow off his or her emotions, if you choose to continue the encounter to resolve the conflict. You can refer back to previous chapters for specific details on dealing with emotions. Here are a few more points to keep in mind:

- Try not to take the other person's behavior personally. A difficult person is likely to use the same kinds of behavior with everybody to satisfy his or her needs. So remind yourself of this to help you avoid any feelings of self-blame and to feel less upset yourself.
- Notice if you are finding this person difficult because he or she reminds you of someone with whom you had bad experiences in the past (i.e.: Does this person remind you of your overprotective mother; your older brother who always put you down, etc.?). If so, attempt to separate your reactions to this person now from your reactions to that other person in the past by reminding yourself that this person is not the person from your past.
- Use creative visualization, affirmations, or other calming techniques to cool yourself down and release the emotions you feel.
- Use communication or listening techniques to let the other person release some of his or her emotions.
- If you are becoming emotionally upset because you are picking up the difficult person's particular way of viewing the world (i.e.: you are beginning to feel down because you are with a perennial pessimist; to feel hostile because you are with a hostile-aggressive person; to feel trapped because you are with a rigid perfectionist, etc.), notice that you are doing this, so you can stop yourself. Remind yourself that you are letting yourself see things from another person's point of view, and that while you are open

to understanding this view, you are not that person; you have your own viewpoint. So distance yourself from the other person; repeat to yourself again and again, "I am not that person. I have my own way of seeing the world," or some such statement. Then, as you do, breathe out and let go. You are letting go of that person's point of view and retrieving your own.

Thinking About Why the Difficult Person Is Being Difficult

The key here is to think about what the difficult person may need or want that is leading him or her to be difficult. What are that person's goals, and how is being difficult helping to achieve that end? By assessing the person's needs, you'll be better able to decide whether you want to address them. It may be that you'll have to, as when that person is in a higher power position than you (such as your boss) and you don't want to leave your own position at present. Or this assessment of needs might convince you that you don't really want to deal with the situation at all. You can walk away from it more knowledgeably than if you just decide to tune out and turn off without knowing much more than the person's difficult scenario.

For example, suppose you are confronted by a silent clam type with whom you've been friends, but who suddenly seems very distant. You feel like something may have happened, but you are not sure what. When you see each other, you feel like this person doesn't want to talk to you. But why? You aren't sure, and you are starting to feel more and more angry and frustrated. One approach might be simply to say forget it, and avoid the situation yourself. If the other person isn't going to tell you what's going on, then too bad. You're not going to play mind- reader, and you can just walk away and go on with your life. And perhaps that might feel comfortable for you.

But on the other hand, this person might have been a valuable friend. Maybe the person is acting this way because he or she is upset or embarrassed about something that has nothing to do with you. Or maybe this person is simply afraid to confront you with a complaint about what really is bothering him or her, because he or she feels it might be difficult to deal with the anger or other feelings released by the encounter. It might be worth it to try to reach these underlying needs by showing you are eager to be supportive and non-judgmental, and by encouraging the person to talk. Probing and paying attention to needs isn't guaranteed to open the person up. But it is a direct and thoughtful approach, and the short time it takes to try might certainly prove worth the effort.

This method can be useful in encounters with any kind of person, but it is particularly helpful in dealing with a difficult person. What makes a person difficult, after all, is his or her special needs. In everyday conflicts, people certainly have needs that motivate them. But often these needs are situational, or are motivated by common desires for prestige, belonging, achievement, financial gain, and the like (such as the desire for a higher ranking title and more responsibility at work). With difficult people, needs are commonly more buried or more tied up with past losses and frustrations (such as the superaggressive person who is trying to cover up underlying feelings of shyness; or the yes-buter who is not used to success or questions his or her own self-worth). You may not be able to play psychiatrist, or you may not want to. But if you at least offer the person a supportive and friendly listener, you may go a long way towards helping the person understand his or her own needs. You may even find that the difficult person is suddenly not being difficult anymore, for he or she has found in you a person to trust and cooperate with instead.

Using Communication To Get to the Root of the Difficulty

Frequently, people are difficult because communication gaps lead them to have wrong assumptions or misunderstandings about something, so they act out of fear or distrust. Communication problems can occur with a person who is normally easy to get along with and lead to conflict. But with a difficult person, these communication problems become even more serious; they become magnified because the difficult person tends to overreact, and an obstacle becomes a mountain.

An example is the kind of miscommunications that sometimes occur at work. Say, as a result of mixed messages, a worker thinks a fellow employee is trying to sabotage her own efforts and make her look bad to the supervisor. The mid-year reviews are coming up, and she thinks the other employee wants to increase his chances for a promotion. In an ordinary situation, the worker might get angry, confront the other employee with her suspicions, or perhaps engineer some reverse sabotage. The sparring back and forth might seem like office politics as usual.

However, if this kind of situation occurs for the "difficult" person, he is apt to be much more sensitive to any perceived slights or attacks, and accordingly respond even more intensely to create a far more explosive situation. In fact, the difficult person might even use his reputation as being a difficult person in order to get his way and get others to back down. For instance, the aggressive-hostile type of person might respond by an explosion of anger, threats, dire predictions, heated accusations, and the like—just what makes others feel very intimidated. Or the clam type might retreat even more into his shell, making it a point to show that he won't even deign to speak to the employee he believes to be at the root of his problems.

Thus, with difficult people it can be especially critical to try to clear out the communication channels, so the correct communications can go through. It may be harder to do this and you may have to make more of an effort to get your message across than with a non-difficult person (for example, by being more insistent, more conciliatory, more respectful, more solicitous, or whatever it takes). But if you really do want to resolve the conflict, rather than just avoid the whole thing, it may be worth the attempt. You may find you are able to cut through the layer of emotional armor, distrust, and fear that help to make the difficult person difficult in the first place. And once you do, you may find the difficult person is not so difficult anymore, at least with you.

Overcoming the Responsibility Trap
With a Difficult Person

Difficult people can be particularly sensitive about issues of blame and responsibility. They may be more likely to seek to blame others, or more vociferous in their accusations. Or they may be more defensive if they think someone else is blaming them, and they may even act this way if they think they really are at fault, but don't want to admit it to others or themselves. In fact, one difficult type is the *chronic blamer*, who is eager to find fault when something goes wrong and, of course, put the accusing finger on someone else. It's as if the blamer sees blaming as the key to solving the problem. But pointing fingers usually does no such thing, since it does more than assigning responsibility. It additionally puts down or demeans the person who has supposedly done the wrong, and that just makes the person feel bad. He or she will probably respond with a correspondingly defensive response (e.g.: "I didn't do it ... she did," or "Maybe I did it, but I was only following orders."). Alternatively, you may sometimes encounter the *martyr*, who wants to take the blame for everything, and can cause as many problems. In taking the blame for something he didn't do, or making his own wrongdoing seem even worse, the martyr acts as if self-debasement will itself correct or atone for the problem. He might hope that others will like or approve of him even more, because he has taken on this scapegoat role. But that doesn't solve the underlying problem either.

The problem with both martyr and chronic blamer is that they tend to dramatize and thereby escalate any conflict, by overlaying the basic problem with their own personal needs. For example, the blamer typically feels he or she must always be right, and to support this feeling throughout a conflict makes others seem wrong. By contrast, the martyr typically wants desperately to be liked, so he or she will step into the scapegoat role so everyone else will feel relieved of the blame and have the martyr to thank. To make things worse, you may find that these difficult types combine this behavior with other types of difficult roles. For instance, the hostile-aggressive steamroller or exploder may easily become the blamer and yell and scream and blame everyone else, while the silent clam may just as easily slip into the martyr role by letting everyone else dump on him or her without saying anything to resist.

Thus, with a difficult person, it is especially important to avoid getting stuck in the responsibility trap. Try not to let the discussion focus on assigning responsibility for the problem. One way to do this might be to move away from a discussion about the past and more towards one concerning the future, in order to emphasize the need to look past the causes and towards solutions. You might say yes, this happened, and yes, you (or the other person, or perhaps still others) may have some responsibility for what occurred. But now that doesn't matter so much. What's really important now is to focus on what you both can do to achieve a resolution.

In other words, you want to neutralize the difficult person's concerns about past responsibility and take the initiative yourself in directing the person's awareness to the future. This strategy may seem to fly in the face of the need to get people to accept responsibility if they are at fault in order to get them to take some action to correct the problem. Also, it may seem to contradict the importance of acknowledging responsibility yourself when you recognize your own contribution to the conflict. But if you are dealing with a difficult person who is determined to blame others or take the blame himself, it may be better simply to deflect this urge by downplaying the importance of taking responsibility. Instead, stress the need to think about how to resolve the conflict now, regardless of who may have been responsible for it in the past. In doing this, you may ultimately get a blamer to accept responsibility or a martyr to let it go, but you do so by sidestepping the issue. People may reach the appropriate resolution of taking or not taking responsibility, but they no longer have to think consciously about the role they are taking. Rather, they can just act.

Choosing the Style of Conflict To Suit the Difficult Person

You might also want to take into consideration the type of difficult person you are dealing with in choosing the appropriate conflict style to use. As previously noted, the five basic styles are competition, accommodation, compromise, collaboration, and avoidance.

In dealing with a difficult person, you may just want to choose avoidance, because the person is so hard to deal with. You want to walk away from the blamer, the exploder, the steamroller, the perennial pessimist, the complainer, or any of the other difficult types. But there are many cases in which you can't do this. You might work with or for these people, or you may find that a difficult person has something you want or need. For example, one time I was involved in a writing project with an especially difficult person, who I would characterize as a combination blamer/complainer/pessimist. To a great extent, these behaviors were triggered by the newness of the project, since the man had never written a book before. He was constantly worried that things would go wrong and he didn't trust me, the publisher, or the book industry generally, though he desperately wanted to have a book. Whatever the cause, the man was very difficult to deal with; I felt like I was constantly walking on eggshells since almost anything could set him off. But I had made a commitment to finish the book, would get paid for it when I did, and the book was already accepted by the man's prospective publisher. So I found ways to calm him down, reassure him, and acknowledge his fears and concerns. In essence, I chose to be accommodating. Any efforts I made to try to work out a compromise only triggered the man's underlying suspicions and fears about being taken advantage of in a field he didn't know and didn't trust. And collaboration was out of the question because his emotions were so close to the surface that it was unrealistic to sit down and try to negotiate anything. Thus, for all practical purposes, accommodation was the only alternative, except for walking away from the situation entirely. Because I placed a greater priority on completing the project than avoiding it, accommodation is the method I chose.

You may often find that your choice with a difficult person is between those two alternatives, avoidance and accommodation. A difficult person tends to use his difficult behavior to get his way. The steamroller steamrolls, the complainer complains, the exploder explodes, and so forth, because he expects others to go meekly along with what he wants in order to avoid the conflict. If the issues involved in the conflict aren't that important to you, it may be worth it either to walk away or to give in. At least that way you can preserve the peace, or continue to work together on the other person's terms.

On the other hand, if you are willing to take some time and the issue is important enough to you, you might be able to use some other strategies to get more of what you want—most notably through compromise or collaboration. But then you need to take into consideration the special needs which make the person difficult, so you can work out some kind of alternative through a compromise or collaboration arrangement which addresses them. For example, suppose you work in an office where you feel one of your co-workers is constantly finding reasons to put you down. She criticizes your work to others, tells the boss that you didn't do things you did, and you even suspect her of misdirecting your memos and mail, though you can't prove this and you're afraid to lodge any accusations. You might be tempted to avoid this person or to back down in meetings to avoid an open war, which might poison the atmosphere even more. However, if you take some time to dig beneath the surface, you might be able to uncover what is really wrong and find some peaceful compromise or collaborative solution.

You might even turn this difficult person into an ally, or a friend. For instance, if this person is acting a certain way towards you because she is jealous, you want to deal with the jealousy; if you remind her of someone who has hurt her in the past, you want to deal with that. One way to reach these underlying problems is to try to find some time to talk about them. If the person seems resistant to talking to you, you might start with gestures to provide the basis for peace—go out of your way to say a friendly hello, offer some tickets around the office and make it a point to include this person in your offer, and so on. In short, try to diffuse the person's underlying reasons for being difficult. To do so, it can help to be supportive, empathic, and friendly yourself, to encourage the person to be pleasant to you in return. Sure, you may feel motivated to avoid or squash this person who has been so difficult. That's the effect difficult people have. But if you fight against any such initial tendencies, you may be able to get to the root of the problem. And then, having cleared the air, having undercut the person's reason for being difficult, you can proceed to find a resolution that is satisfying for you both.

Dealing With Common Types of Difficult People

While the general principles just described may be useful for dealing with difficult people generally, certain strategies may be particularly helpful with certain types of difficult people.

Following are a sample of these,[4] though remember that any difficult person may have a combination of these traits (for example, a person who explodes may also be a silent clam at times). The key is to remain flexible, and adapt your approach to the particular person, his or her underlying needs, and your own priorities in resolving or walking away from the situation.

The Steamroller/Sherman Tank Types. These are the people who come on like gangbusters, thinking that if they push others around they will get their way, since others will simply back down. Also, they may act like this because they are convinced they are right, and are determined to show this to others. At the same time, some of these types may fear they might be shown up for being wrong. This is a scary prospect, for it may undermine the steamroller's image of himself. If the issue's not particularly important to you, your best bet is probably to avoid or accommodate. Give the person a wide berth, or give in to small things to calm the person down. If you choose another tack, it's a good idea to begin by letting the person let off steam. Then calmly and surely present your own point of view, but avoid making the person feel wrong, since this is sure to inspire another round of hostile responses. Picture your role as that of a peacemaker who is above the fray. Meet the person's fury with your own inner serenity and calm: this will help the other person put aside his or her aggression, and you can work things out from there.

The Undercover Attacker/Sniper Type. This is the secret saboteur who tries to cut others down with behind-the-stage machinations, cutting remarks, and other veiled shows of aggression. He or she commonly thinks this behavior is fully justified; someone else has done something wrong, and he or she is a kind of secret avenger setting things right. Yet he or she acts behind the scenes because he or she doesn't feel enough power to act openly. The battle is like fighting with a guerrilla soldier.

Again, if you decide that avoidance or learning to live with these attacks is not for you, the best way to deal with this type

---

[4] These include some of the types identified by Bramson in his book *Coping with Difficult People.*

of person is first to surface the attack and then to get to the underlying reasons. Let the attacker know you are onto him by saying something like: "Was that meant as a put down?" If the undercover attacker tries to deny it, present your evidence. You want to keep your cool as you do this, so the attacker doesn't feel *you* are attacking aggressively, which might only lead to an open battle. As you continue to identify the intended undercover attacks, the undercover attacker will finally realize you've got him revealed—it's like you've blown his cover. He'll know he must either stop the attacks or openly justify them. And once the attacks are surfaced, you can see what's really bothering the person and find a way to deal with the problem.

The Angry Child/Exploder. This kind of person doesn't just get angry; he gets furious and explodes like a child having a tantrum. Commonly, the person who does this feels very fearful and frustrated, and this is his or her way of gaining control. For example, the husband may erupt when he feels insanely jealous about something he thinks his wife is doing and fears losing her or losing control; or the employer may blow up as a way of getting an unruly staff back into line.

If you are on the receiving end of such a tirade, the first principle to use to avoid escalating things further (unless you decide to walk away from all this) is to let the person finish yelling and screaming, until he or she has finished venting the burst of emotion. Or reassure the person that you are listening and are there ready to be responsive to calm him. The idea is to help the person feel he is still in control, while calming him down. Then, when the person is calm again, just act like the person is an ordinary, reasonable person, as if the tantrum incident never happened. Politely and calmly offer to talk about the problem. You may find the person is embarrassed and apologetic about the yelling and screaming incident. If so, just accept his apologies to help him feel better. But otherwise it's probably best to shift the focus away from the incident, since the person is likely to be eager to forget it happened. Once back in control, he would like to be seen as a responsible, rational adult.

The Complainer. There are really two types of complainers: the realistic complainer, and the paranoid who has complaints about imaginary slights. In either case, the complainer is frequently griping about something and blaming others—either specific identifiable people or the world, generally—for all manner of wrongs. Sometimes, the complainer may simply unload on you as a willing ear. But at other times, you may find yourself at the brunt of the complainer's attacks, berated for something you did or something he blames you for doing.

If the complainer is talking about someone else, a common reaction may be to tune the person out. Alternatively, you may want to argue back and point out that what the complainer is saying is untrue or unhelpful. But neither approach will really solve the basic problem. In the first case, the complainer will have found one more topic to talk about: you and your failure to listen. And in the second, case the complainer is likely just to get defensive, because you're attacking and because you haven't really responded to his or her complaints.

Instead, the key to dealing with the complainer is to begin by listening. It doesn't matter whether the complaints seem true or unfounded. The complainer wants desperately to be heard. That's why the complainer is constantly complaining—because he thinks no one is listening or taking him seriously or doing what he says. His complaints usually arise out of frustration and a sense of not having any power. By listening, you help to give the person a feeling of power and a place to discharge his frustration.

You should acknowledge or validate the complainer by showing that you have understood what he is saying; perhaps by repeating in other words a capsule description of what he has said. Then, once the complainer has poured out his basic complaint, seek some closure. You might even think of yourself as a Small Claims judge hearing a petitioner present a case. If the person starts to repeat himself, as complainers often do, you can calmly and respectfully interrupt to stop the person from running on and on. Try to shift the person into a problem-solving mode. What does the person want to *do* about the problem? Are there others who might help solve the problem? If he is blaming you for something, what can you do now together to find some resolution? In short, you want to acknowledge the person's complaint, then move on.

Incidentally, in acknowledging, you don't have to agree with the complaint. If it's true, sure, agree. But if not, just point out that you understand, and remain neutral. Emphasize that now that the complaint is clear, the question is what to do about it. You may have to shift the conversation back to the process of solving the problem more than once. But if you can break this pattern of complaining again and again, you can deal with the conflict by discussing it and thinking about realistic solutions where possible. Or if the complainer is mistaken in his complaints, you can help the complainer see the mistake once he feels understood. Of course, if the complainer keeps complaining and you feel like you are going around in circles, you can always give up. But at least you have given it a shot.

The Quiet Clams and Silent Types. These quiet types can be quiet for any number of reasons, and what's especially frustrating about dealing with them is that you just don't know. The key to resolving a conflict, unless you want to avoid the issue entirely, is to get the person to open up. You might have some suspicions (such as the person being angry about some incident but not wanting to tell you), but it's not a good idea to act on that premise. If you are wrong, you can end up even further escalating the conflict.

To help get things out in the open you might ask some open-ended questions, inviting more than a yes, no, or nod response. If you get a brief reply, ask some follow-up questions, such as: "What's your feeling about that?" or "What happened that led you to feel that way?" Also, if you have any suspicions about what is wrong, and the person doesn't volunteer the information himself, you might share these suspicions to see if they are correct (e.g.: "I thought you might be avoiding me because you felt I slighted you at the office party.") Keep probing or encouraging the person to speak, and even acknowledge that it may be difficult for the person to share his feelings (something like, "I know you may not like to talk about this, but if we can get this situation out in the open, then we can deal with it and try to resolve it.").

Show that you are willing to be supportive and empathic no matter what the person says. Frequently, clams clam up because they don't want to hurt other people's feelings, have been taught not to share their own feelings, want to avoid confrontations, feel their own opinions aren't valued, or are just generally shy. Thus, it's particularly important to validate, support, and affirm this person. Show that whatever he or she says, you won't get angry, won't put that person down, won't be hurt, etc. Rather, you truly value what he or she says and really do want to hear it, even if you disagree or don't like what he or she says.

It's easy to become impatient with these people, because it's so hard to get a response. But if the issue is worth it, stick with it. Eventually the clam may open up, like a reluctant oyster finally giving up its pearl. When that time comes, provide positive reinforcement. Show you appreciate that the person is talking to you, whether or not you agree or like what the person is saying. And if the person should pause in responding, give him or her plenty of time to reply, so you don't cut off the response. It can be tempting to start talking yourself to fill up the silence, but then you take the clam off the hook. Keep up the pressure, like you're patiently nudging a stuck object out of a hole. As you see progress, continue to acknowledge it, to encourage more.

At the same time, be sensitive to how far you can go. If you see the clam suddenly digging in to resist some more, you may want to give the problem a rest. If so, just thank the clam for whatever communication you have gained so far, back off, and if it seems profitable, try to arrange some time to meet again. You may not be able to resolve everything in one shot, but if you've gotten an opening, at least it's a start. Later, you can pick up your attempts to work out the problem from here.

Super-Agreeables Who Don't Come Through. Super-agreeables can seem pretty nice, not difficult at all, because they go out of their way to be helpful and liked. But at times this can be the problem: you count on a super-agreeable person who agrees to things, but then doesn't perform. A co-worker agrees to take on some responsibility, but then doesn't; a friend agrees to do something with you, and then finds some reason to cancel at the last minute, while you're left stuck.

Assuming you think it worthwhile to continue relating to this person, the key to resolving the conflict is to show that you really do want the person to be truthful. Insist that you want to know what the person *really* thinks, and only want the person to do what he really can or will do. You want to emphasize that what bothers you is not whether the person agrees to things or not, but the person's lack of follow-through on what he or she does agree to do.

Your stress should be on the person telling the truth, no matter what. This means showing that you will support and approve of the person for doing so. Typically, a person agrees to more than he should out of a fear of telling the truth and not being liked. You want to provide the underlying support to help the person be truthful. You may have to provide this reassurance several times, until the person really feels comfortable and protected in sharing the facts with you, or in saying no.

Once you are able to get the facts out or see what the super-agreeable really thinks, you can talk honestly about any problems between you. Then again, once the super-agreeable says what he really thinks, the main problem will disappear: you'll know where the person stands and what he will do, and you won't feel the let-down anymore that comes from his lack of follow-through.

Naysayers and Perrenial Pessimists. It can be very discouraging to be around these negative types who think that things are bound to go wrong and are constantly worrying about things or saying no. Optimally, you may want to avoid such people, because they bring you down with them. If you can't , a good approach is to try to uncover the person's underlying fear leading to the negativity in any particular situation. At the same time, concentrate on not getting sucked into seeing the world from the negativist's point of view in order to maintain your own optimism.

In dealing with the person's fear, you might keep in mind that pessimists frequently feel a lack of control. They feel things will just happen to them, usually bad. Psychologists sometimes refer to this syndrome as a condition of "learned helplessness." Another way to put it is to suggest that the person has a "locus of control" outside himself, meaning that he sees himself as a victim or pawn in the hands of outside forces. Thus, it can help the person feel more in control by showing him the ways in which he does have some ability to change what he doesn't like, or to prevent things from going wrong. For example, if the person is coming up with reasons as to why something won't work, you might just listen quietly for a while, to acknowledge the person's concerns and show you understand. But then, show there is another point of view, and describe realistic alternatives. If you can, use specific examples of past successes under similar circumstances, or at least offer your optimistic view that something still can be done. You might ay something like: "Well, let's at least try this new approach. We haven't tried it yet, and I feel if we give it a chance, it may work."

Frequently, these negative types may also try to "yes, but" you. Whatever you propose, they come up with a reason why that won't work. Initially, you might try to answer with some hopeful alternatives. But then, if you see the "yes, but" pattern emerging, call the negative person on it. Point out that every time you suggest anything, the other person comes up with a reason why it won't work; you wonder if the person is open to *any* alternatives. Confronted by this honesty, the person may well back down.

On the other hand, if you see that the negative person is strongly invested in his position that things won't work, it may be better not to argue. It would be hard to talk him out of it, particularly since you aren't sure whether the alternatives you are suggesting will work or not, and he *is* certain. You might work your way around the negative person's conviction simply by suggesting that even if he is correct, it might be worth trying your ideas anyway. Tell him to humor you: maybe the ideas will suggest more productive approaches, maybe they'll provide at least a partial solution, and maybe they'll just prove the negative person right.

Alternatively, without confronting the negative person at all, you might try to come up with evidence that will lead the negative person to recognize his pessimistic error independently. There might even be something that can be done to counter his underlying fear.

As you engage in all these attempts to break through the negative person's negative shield, monitor your own reactions. Dealing with negative people can be very draining. They sap your own energy and threaten to pull you into their negative perspective. If this starts happening, gently pull yourself away from the attempt to resolve the conflict, or ask for a breather. It may be that you just cannot resolve the problem, though you gave it your best shot.

On the other hand, if you do begin to see some movement in the person's attitude, it can be worth it to stick with the resolution process or perhaps take a brief break and return. You may not be able to change the person's overall way of looking at the world, but at least you may be able to shift his way of looking at this particular situation. And that's all the change you need.

The Indecisives and Stallers. People who can't make a decision or keep putting one off are often afraid of results, unwilling to take responsibility for the outcome, or scared that any decision will hurt someone. If it's hard for them to say no, they'll keep putting things off. This behavior can be very frustrating, especially if you're in a situation where your action awaits the person's decision (e.g.: you work for an indecisive and aren't sure what to do next; you are trying to plan some joint activity with a friend or spouse). If you aren't already in conflict about the action in question, the indecision and stalling can itself lead to a conflict.

One approach is simply to take a more forceful position yourself (i.e.: the competitive approach to conflict), and assert the decision you want. Do this diplomatically if it's appropriate for you to make the decision at all. Let the indecisive feel comfortable with your control, or even feel as if he or she contributed to the process. The indecisive is likely to go along with a good proposal and may be relieved the decision has been taken care of. The danger is that the indecisive may just go along with the decision to keep the peace, but retain misgivings. This could set the stage for more conflict later over the outcome.

If you really do want or need the indecisive's decision, the first thing you need to do is find out why the indecisive is hesitating, so you can get rid of this block. The indecisive may not be open with that informtion. Sometimes he or she is trying to avoid hurt feelings by stalling. And sometimes that person doesn't even know the reason, but just has some vague unconscious fear about deciding. One key to getting the indecisive to talk is to show you are supportive and won't be hurt by whatever the indecisive decides. You just want to know what the person really thinks, whatever that is. Once you have surfaced what's really going on for the indecisive, you'll have a more solid basis for trying to resolve problems or make joint decisions. You are no longer in the dark battling some hidden reason which is causing the person to hold back.

Crazymakers. These people can be particularly unnerving as they bend and break the rules of ordinary human behavior—rooted in expectation and trust—and leave you feeling like you're slipping and sliding in the mud. When you can't avoid dealing with a person who is behaving this way, the first step is to recognize that this is happening. Don't let yourself get sucked into this person's view of the world or a particular situation: you will just internalize the contradictory or unmeetable expectations and feel crazy yourself. Rather, from this point of view of awareness, try to make the other person see those contradictions. Then, try to find out what underlying factors are causing the person to act or think like this. For example, suppose a person has repeatedly set up meetings with you, but has cancelled each of them at the last minute. You're beginning to wonder if the person really wants to have this meeting. Rather than accepting the person's bland apologies and setting another meeting, you might ask the person point blank if there is some reason he or she doesn't want to meet with you now, and if so, can you talk about that.

When you do point out contradictions and try to talk about the underlying reasons, it can help to wait for an interlude when things are calm, so you can raise these points diplomatically. For example, if someone is yelling at you for not having met his or her impossible expectations, this might not be the best time to confront that person with the problem. You are likely to make the other person defensive or even angrier, because he or she may feel accused. Instead, aim for a time between incidents when you can broach the topic, or perhaps try when the person first approaches you with impossible expectations. At that time, describe the problem in a calm and neutral way, so you appeal to the person's reason and encourge his or her involvement in finding a solution.

For example, you might say something like: "Look, I'd really like to be able to do what you want ... [you fill in the goal], but there are some obstacles towards being able to do this ... [you fill in the obstacles]. This is what I see as the problem ... [you describe the contradictions]. So I hope we can work together to try to resolve this. Maybe we could ... [say what you suggest].

Crazymaking is harder to deal with when it occurs in a close personal relationship between parents and children, spouses, and lovers. There the process is more subtle and more tied in with underlying needs. Think of the perfectionist parent who sets impossible high standards for his or her child. When the child ultimately fails, the parent makes the mistake of blaming. In such relationships, passions and stakes can be much higher. However, where it's possible to deal with these situations without calling in some professional help, the basic principles are the same. You want to start by recognizing the conflicted expectations that lie at the root of the crazymaking. Once these are clear, try to distance yourself emotionally from the situation so you feel calm and neutral and don't take the other person's point of view. In this calm and neutral state, you want to find a time when you can point out the contradictions if you can to the other person. If the other person is willing to acknowledge and accept these, you can go on to the final stage—working out a mutually productive solution together.

And what if you can't solve the problem? What if the other person isn't willing to listen or work things out? And what if your attempts to resolve things only make the person angrier and angrier? It may be you can't do anything, and your only alternative is to fall back to avoidance (avoid the person, end the relationship, quit the job) or you might choose to continue suffering in silence, knowing the person has given you contradictory instructions or may let you down once again, because you feel preserving the relationship or job is worth the price.

Being aware of the problem may not end the crazymaking, but it will let you set your own priorities and choose your course of action. It will also help you feel secure in your own sanity and competence in the face of impossible demands.

Dealing With Other Difficult Types

What about the perfectionists, secret forts, innocent liars, resentful altruists, game players, and other difficult types? As in many of the situations already described, the key is to get the problem behavior out on the table. On your own or together, try to identify the underlying reasons or needs causing the behavior.

Once you have clear reasons or needs in sight, you'll have a better idea of how to meet them and get around the block. Ideally, you'll be able to overcome the problem behavior and then deal with any further conflicts without that block standing in the way.

Specifically, you want to find out why the perfectionist is so demanding and then point out why this behavior isn't necessary or is counterproductive in this case. Let the secret fort know you want to know what's really wrong, because you sense that he or she is bothered by something. Tell the secret liar that you feel he or she may not be completely candid with you (though don't call him or her on "lying," which is apt to only provoke anger or further lies), and then empathize you really need to know what the person thinks. Likewise, encourage the resentful altruist to express his true feelings. And call the game players on their games—though again, the key is diplomacy. Let them know you know what they're doing, but do it nicely, in a friendly tone, so they don't get mad. You might tell the "yes, but-er": "Well, it sounds like everytime I make a suggestion, you find a reason why it won't work. Do you really want to solve this problem? If so, maybe we can look for some other alternatives. But if not, maybe we should go on to talk about something else."

In Summary

When you encounter a difficult person, you'll want to use strategy tailored to address that person's particular behavior problem. This strategy will vary from type to type, but you can use these key points as your guide:

1) Become aware yourself that the person is being difficult and note the type of difficult behavior he is exhibiting.
2) Distance yourself from this behavior or this person's point of view, so you don't get sucked into his orientation but can stay calm and neutral.
3) If you decide not to avoid the situation entirely, try to talk to the person and find out his underlying reasons for being difficult.

4) Try to find a way of satisfying those underlying reasons or needs.

5) Use mutual problem solving to resolve any other conflicts that become clear once the person's difficult behavior has been identified and is eliminated or controlled.

Part III

Using Your Intuition To Discover New Possibilities

11

Coming Up With
Alternatives and Solutions

You've defined your problem. You're willing to work through it and consider alternative solutions. But how exactly do you go about finding those alternatives? This chapter can help you. One method you'll learn to consider is brainstorming. You can brainstorm alone or with others, following a few strict rules to generate ideas very freely. A second method will help you look within and ask your inner expert for suggestions. Both methods help you maximize your creativity and apply it to your search for a resolution. Either or both methods should give you a long list of alternative solutions to choose from. These methods can also be used to confirm—or reject—ideas you already have.

Brainstorming

When you brainstorm, you try to come up with as many possible solutions as you can without trying to decide what is appropriate. By not trying to edit or control your thoughts, you unleash your creativity.

Of course, eventually you'll want to think realistically about your ideas. That's the second stage of the brainstorming process. But in the first stage, you just let your intuitive part come up with ideas as quickly as it can. Wait until later for the editor to come in to choose and select.

Creative artists and inventors use this very same process to develop their ideas. So do I, as a writer. In the first phase, I simply sit down at the typewriter and let my creativity go without trying to say: "Okay, this has to be perfect." And then in the second phase, I do the editing.

The reason you don't want to do any selection or editing in the first stage is that this can block the process. If you think something should be a certain way in advance, you'll inhibit your creativity. This can occur because the creative part of yourself gets the idea that it has to come up with a fully finished and realized concept, and a barrier of fear goes up. The creative flow shuts down.

It's the same in dealing with conflicts, both with other people and within yourself. There are many different ways to resolve any particular conflict. But sometimes people get stuck because they look for the one perfect resolution, and feel there are only certain ways of achieving it. Popular advice columns such as "Dear Abby" only perpetuate this notion. They propose the "right" solution. The truth is that if you describe the same situation to other people, you will find as many proposed solutions as there are people, and sometimes more.

So open your mind to possibilities. Remember that there is no set way of dealing with any conflict. People have different ways of approaching each problem, depending on personalities, interests, circumstances, and many other factors. Let yourself go in brainstorming to tap into all the possibilities your creative mind can generate. In the second editing phase of the process, you can select the approach or approaches you feel are the most appropriate for resolving the conflict.

Brainstorming on Your Own

If you are brainstorming on your own, a good way to come up with ideas is to take a sheet of paper or a notebook and set aside about 10 minutes for stage one. Then, in a quiet place free of distractions, focus on the problem and as quickly as possible think of as many ideas as you can for solving it. You might even imagine that someone else has come to you with this problem, and you are giving this person advice.

As the ideas come to you, write them down. Write quickly so you don't lose your train of thought. Don't give yourself time to think about whether the ideas are silly or impractical. You don't want to edit or censor them now in any way. You can choose the good ones later.

If the ideas don't come at first, keep concentrating for the time period you have set. You'll find that focusing your attention will help to get the ideas started, and then one idea can start the flow of more. You might also consider adding onto or modifying the ideas that come, to think of even more possibilities, or even think about opposites or variations on a theme (such as: don't just talk to that person, talk to someone else; try writing to someone as well as talking …). However, when you think of corollaries, you don't want to think of "insteads ofs," which might put down a former idea. Your goal is to think of as many ideas as possible. It's unlikely that you'll have no ideas. Should you find yourself slowing down, then stop at the end of the time limit. But if you find you are getting all sorts of ideas, keep going as long as they are flowing freely.

When you're sure you have finished with the idea generation process, go over your ideas. Rate them from 1—or very good—to 5—not very good at all; 3 can mean neutral, or that you're not sure yet. Afterwards, you can take the ideas you rated the most highly and put them into practice. If you need further clarification on how to apply a particular idea, you can always go through the brainstorming process again, focusing on ways to make the idea work.

It's possible you'll find that brainstorming on your own doesn't work. Sometimes it's hard to get the distance and freedom you need to be creative when you're in the midst of a problem. If you are feeling really stuck, try brainstorming with another person or in a small group for a fresh perspective on your problem.

Brainstorming With Others

Sometimes brainstorming with others is just the thing you need to get unstuck when you feel you have exhausted your own ideas on what to do. In this case, you might get together with a friend or associate, or form a small group of six to eight people. You might even draft some dinner guests into a quick brainstorming session. In fact, if the others would like to brainstorm for solutions to their own problems, you might take turns doing this. It'll make for a novel dinner party at least!

To begin this process, you (or whoever's problem is being brainstormed) should have a sheet of paper and a pencil to record any ideas. If you have a large board everyone can see, so much the better. It's also a good idea to sit in a circle if you can. Each person's contribution will take on equal value that way (although don't write names next to ideas when you list them: this frees everyone to be free and spontaneous. Besides, listing names takes too much time).

Then, describe your conflict situation. Use the first person, if you feel comfortable doing this. Or if this makes you uncomfortable, describe the situation in the third person, as if it happened to someone else. In describing the situation, try to be as neutral as possible in presenting the facts. You want to give everyone else an objective picture of the situation, and you don't want to advance any preconceptions about what you think the solution should be. Describe your perspective, and then try to describe the other party's perspective. Before the problem solving begins, allow anyone to ask questions to clarify what the problem is. Make sure you keep it to factual, clarifying questions. Don't let yourself get sucked into subjective or accusing questions ("Why didn't you _____," or "Were you aware of that person's feelings about _____?").

Once everyone has a clear understanding of the conflict, you can go on to the problem solving stage. You can do this in one of three ways: 1) let everyone else brainstorm alone at first, while you just write down ideas and say nothing (you can then do some on-the-spot brainstorming yourself to contribute your ideas when the others are finished); 2) you start brainstorming first and write down ideas while others listen (you'll let others brainstorm afterwards, while you just listen and write); and 3) you and everyone else can all brainstorm at the same time, and you write down any ideas that come up as before. You might try experimenting with these different methods to find out which is most comfortable and productive for you.

Whichever approach you use, whoever is brainstorming should throw out as many suggestions as possible. There's no need to go in any particular order. Just contribute ideas as you think of them. Feel free to piggy-back or expand on an idea you have heard; but don't criticize or put down any other ideas, because that can interfere with the creativity flow by making others feel self-conscious. You want to avoid being judgmental so others won't be afraid to make suggestions. The secret to successful brainstorming is that everything is possible, and nothing should be judged wrong, ridiculous, or unworkable in advance.

By the same token, if you are listening to other people come up with ideas for you, don't make any comments about why it won't work or how you've tried it before. That means no "yes, buts" or "but I tried that." Again, such comments will only interrupt the creative flow. Simply write down whatever people say, and you can always eliminate the unworkable or previously tried ideas later.

In writing down these comments, you just need to write enough to trigger your memory. You don't have to write everything down. There's no need to slow down the process for taking notes. Just record as much as you can at the time.

Once the first stage of the process is over, go through the list of ideas you have recorded. That's the time to choose what seems to make the most sense to you as solutions to the conflict. To do so, use a rating system from 1 to 5. Put 1 next to those things you most want to do, a 2 next to those you'd like to do if possible. Put a 3 next to the maybes, a 4 for the probably nots, and a 5 for the nos. Then, you can put the more practical and highest priority solution or solutions into practice right away.

Examples of Brainstorming

How well does this brainstorming process work? Here are some representative examples from a workshop which illustrate how people worked through the problems they came in with. They brainstormed as a small group, and all of them came away with some new ideas they could use to resolve their particular conflict.

In one case, a woman was very concerned about getting a new job she wanted. As she described it, it seemed "a dream job," a perfect match with her skills. She was scared, though, because the job was in a new field and she would have to leave her old career. She explained that she had been going through the motions of taking steps towards making the change, such as writing up a resume. "But my fear is a big block," she said, "I'm not afraid to apply for the job, but I'm afraid to put all that energy out and I'm afraid of not getting it. So I may not try as hard as I should or could to really get it." In response, the two men she was brainstorming with had all sorts of suggestions. Since she felt stuck in coming up with new ideas herself, she just listened. Some of the possibilities included:

- Apply for the job; forget about your fear, and just apply for the adventure of it.
- Think of how well you will do in the job when you get it.
- Don't think of this as the only great job opportunity you will get; recognize that there will be many others.
- Think about the other situations you have been in where you have been afraid and things worked out; realize that you will survive this one, too.
- Visualize yourself getting the job: see your employer hiring you enthusiastically, on the spot.
- Think of all the good qualities you have which make you very employable; you'll have more confidence when you interview and will be more likely to get the job
- Think of this job interview as one more step in the learning process; even if you don't get this job, your effort isn't wasted. You'll have prepared yourself, so you're ready for the next job that comes along.

As you can see from this example, brainstorming can be as helpful in dealing with feelings as it can be in coming up with concrete action plans.

Another woman confessed to hating her job, which she felt she had to stick with for another eight months, since she was a teacher and the school term had just started. After a brainstorming session, she too came away with a long list of useful ideas. As she described the problem, she had trouble getting along with the other people at work. She felt like she was working in a prison and felt totally out of synch with the school's philosophy and policies. As she put it:

> I only took the job because I wanted to make enough money to go overseas. But I don't like teaching. How can I avoid having conflicts with people and being critical of where I'm working, since I so hate the job? ...
> I hate it that I have to be there with 25 other teachers and 33 kids. The school feels like a prison and I feel what is happening in the school system is awful. But I have to control my feelings. My real problem is how to stay nice on a job that I hate.

Some of the suggestions she got were quite serious; others more in the nature of humorous, outrageous things she could do to get even or show what she really thought of the system. But even if they weren't especially practical, the ideas helped her to feel better about where she was working. The suggestions helped to release some of the anger and tension she felt, so that even if she would not carry them out, she felt better just thinking about them as possibilities. It was a symbolic release, one she felt she couldn't get in reality. At the same time, once others started throwing out suggestions, this helped her become unstuck in thinking of things she might do. She soon had plenty of her own ideas to add to the list, too. Just to get a flavor of some of the suggestions she received, here is a sampling of the group's brainstorming list.

- Don't talk to the other teachers.
- Eat in the park.
- Stay away from the other teachers.
- Keep your own future goal constantly in mind; the more hope you have about that, the better you can put up with the way things are now.
- Pamper yourself to compensate for what you are suffering now; take bubble baths, or treat yourself to weekly trips to the movies.
- Try to find fulfilling things to do when you are off the job.
- If you find another teacher who seems a little sympathetic, tell him or her what you really think.

- Find a support group of like people who are also in transition and hate their jobs.
- Form a support group for recovering teachers.
- Throw dishes so you feel better.
- Take a picture of the worst person on your job and put that picture on a punching bag, paint circles on it, and throw darts at it.
- Be as playful as you can to have fun with the kids.
- Create a dramatic play about your situation, and have your kids put it on as their class play.
- If there's one teacher you can talk to, whisper quietly: "We can break out of here soon. Pass it on."
- Write the principal's name on dozens of subscription cards to all sorts of magazines and send them in.

The Outcome of Brainstorming

The advantage of using this brainstorming process, particularly with a group of other people, is that it can bring new thinking to a stalemated situation. One person in the group put it this way: "It was like there was a new spark of energy in dealing with this old problem. I might have thought about some of these ideas before, but I didn't do anything with them. The brainstorming provided another way of hearing these ideas said, and that helped to clear up the fog I had experienced about this situation. Now I feel like I can move ahead."

Not all of the proposed solutions may in fact be workable. Some may be offered purely for their humor or to show how creative people can be in coming up with unique, even far-out ideas. But generally, you can expect at least some of the ideas to be useful. In the workshop just described, all of the participants felt they had discovered some new solutions they could put to use.

And sometimes, as participants discovered, just engaging in the process with helpful, supportive people helped them rethink old ideas in a new, workable light. One man in the workshop had this experience. He had a friend whose wife had come down with Parkinson's disease, and for about four years she had been an invalid, with no prospects for getting any better. The man's friend had been struggling with the question of whether he should stay with her during her illness. The friend was feeling more and more depressed by the whole situation, but he felt trapped by his guilt. As the man in the workshop explained:

> After four years, the situation has become overwhelming for him. He comes home from work and he realizes his wife isn't getting any better. Somebody has to take care of her while he's at work. He's not having his own needs met, but he's hesitant to find out what would be good for him.
>
> I had some ideas about what I thought he should do, such as getting a support network of friends or going to support groups for others in this situation. Or he might get friends and neighbors to help with the shopping. Or maybe he should look at his needs in the relationship, and then if he felt he couldn't get them satisfied, maybe he should find some way to break away. But I felt afraid to tell anything to him. I wouldn't know what to say.

However, when the people in his brainstorming group said exactly the things he had been saying, he felt supported in his ideas. He had been hesitant to tell his friend what he really thought, because he thought it might seem like he was urging his friend to be irresponsible. After all, pulling away from this depressing situation meant pulling away entirely or at least to some degree from a woman who was ill and needy. Yet, the man felt like that was what his friend needed to do, and really wanted to do as well to preserve his own sanity and health. He also felt the friend needed support, both in terms of concrete ideas and emotional concern, to help him make the break and do so in a way that would be as easy as possible for the woman. Hearing these ideas echoed by the group in the session helped to give him the push he needed. "Now I feel I'm ready to tell my friend what I really think," he said. "Then, my friend can decide to do what he wants. And I think my support will help him to do what he really needs to do."

Ways of Working With the Brainstorming Process in the Future

One way to make the brainstorming process even more useful to you in the future is to work with it on a regular basis. You can work on resolving various everyday conflicts, or develop general creative ideas. This will help to keep the creative, intuitive part of your mind well-tuned for producing ideas. It's a little like keeping the motor of a car lubricated and turning it on regularly, so it is ready to go when you need it. Five to 15 minutes a day might be good for this purpose. And if you have no particular conflict in your life to work on, just think of some other topic or issue to brainstorm about and let your mind go.

Another way you can use brainstorming is to get together with friends or with contacts at work. Again, you can get their help in resolving a particular problem, or perhaps just practice brainstorming generally. There are all sorts of support groups and interest groups that deal with particular topics. Why not a brainstorming group?

Using Your Inner Expert Process

The Inner Expert Process is another way to tap into your intuitive, creative abilities to resolve conflicts. In this case, instead of trying to come up with as many ideas as possible in a short time, you try to call on your inner self from a relaxed, altered state of consciousness. The techniques of relaxation and visualization should look familiar to you by now; perhaps you have already used them to release conflict, to reduce anger, or to determine which conflict handling style to use in a particular situation. Once again, these inner techniques can give you answers hidden to your everyday, conscious mind.

In using this process, you go within yourself in a semi-trance-like state. This is like a mild hypnosis or an intense meditation, where you are focused yet relaxed. Here, you imagine your inner self to be an expert, and you have a talk with this person. You can do this in a number of ways. For instance, you could see an expert appear on a TV or computer screen; you could meet with somebody in a workshop; you may call on a specific person you already know; you might ask for advice from a teacher you have met with in the past. You can visualize anybody who looks helpful and knowledgeable, since in reality you will be consulting a helpful, knowledgeable part of yourself.

Visualization

The following visualization is designed to help you contact this inner expert within yourself. Eventually, as you work with this inner part of yourself more frequently, you probably will not need to go through the entire process. You'll be able to call on this inner expert almost automatically, just by getting into a relaxed state and asking your inner expert to appear. But initially, this visualization will help. You can read it to yourself and then use it as a general guide; put it on a tape and listen to it; or ask a friend to read it to you while you get relaxed.

Start off by relaxing. Close your eyes, and breathe deeply several times until you feel very comfortable and relaxed. If you know what question or conflict you want to ask about now, let this appear in your mind. If you prefer, you can wait. You'll have a chance during the process to ask the question later, if you are not sure now.

Just focus on your breathing going in and out, in and out, to get calm and relaxed. Feel yourself getting calm and relaxed and very comfortable, as you notice your breathing going in, and out, in, and out. Yet, even as you get relaxed, you'll still be able to hear the sound of my voice and stay alert and awake.

Now I'd like you to imagine yourself in a special place where you feel very comfortable and very safe. It could be your room. It could be a meadow, or a place in the country where you like to go.

See yourself there now. You might see what's around you. Maybe there are books around; maybe you see a computer screen; or maybe you are out in the country and you see trees and grass. Wherever you are, just feel yourself very much a part of the environment.

Then, as you look up, you notice somebody coming towards you. It might be somebody you have seen before, or it might be somebody totally new. Just say hello to this person and know that this person is here to help you and has information to give you.

Invite the person to sit down with you, maybe on a chair, maybe on the grass, maybe on a cushion. And spend a little bit of time getting to know this person. Just ask this person who he or she is. Ask what he or she does. And maybe tell the person a little bit about yourself.

Now, as you talk about yourself, you can tell the person about the problem you have or the conflict situation you are involved in. This problem or conflict may be something you had in mind before you began this experience, or it may be something you are thinking about right now.

Describe the situation to this person, and notice that this person is very sympathetic and understanding and just listens as you talk. Maybe this person has a few questions to ask you to explain the situation in a little more detail. I'll be quiet for a few moments to give you a chance to explain the problem so this person really understands what it is.

(Pause 15-30 seconds.)

And now that you've finished explaining the problem, this person has some answers and suggestions for you. So just listen as this person tells you what to do. These may be ideas you've never heard about before, or maybe these are things you have thought of but aren't sure about. Just listen very receptively. Don't try to judge or evaluate. Just listen to the ideas as they come to you.

(Pause 15-30 seconds.)

Now, if you want, you can ask if this person has any more suggestions. Or if there is something you haven't understood, you can ask this person to explain a little bit more. Again, just listen to the answers.

(Pause 10-15 seconds).

And now this special person is finishing up his or her answer, and if you have another question, you can ask it, or if you have another problem or another conflict you are concerned about, you can ask about this, too.

This time, your special teacher will show you something. You will ask your question, and then, in response, he or she will take you to another place where you will see a screen or a stage, and there you will see your answer played out for you.

So ask your question now. And now just follow your teacher or expert as he or she leads you. Then, in this place you will discover your answer, for you will see it appear in front of you. Maybe it will appear in words, like a headline. Or maybe you will see a little drama playing itself out in front of you on the stage or on the screen as a picture.

Just see what happens. And again, don't try to plan anything. Just receive.

(Pause 15-30 seconds).

And now your teacher or expert is coming to the end of the answer. If you have seen anything in front of you, it starts to fade or vanish. And now it's gone. And then your teacher or expert leads you back to where you started.

Now I'd like you to thank your expert or teacher and start to say goodbye. As you do, know that you can always call on this teacher or expert whenever you want, whenever you have a question or a problem or a conflict and you want some answers. You can either ask a question and get an answer, or you can have your expert take you and show you the answer: whichever you prefer.

So now you see your teacher or expert leaving, and you feel very complete. As you do, I'm going to start counting backwards from five to one, and as I do, you'll become more and more awake and alert, and come back into the room. Five, four, more and more awake. Three, two, almost back. One. And you're back in the room.

Getting Your Answer

When you get your answer, it may come in any number of forms. Some people may get it in the form of very practical, down to earth advice. Others may get it in the form of images or pictures, which may need some interpretation. Some may find their answer from a single expert; others may have multiple experts come to them with advice. Following are some examples of the different ways you might get this help.

Getting Direct Answers

One of the most common ways to expect an answer is in the form of direct advice. This happened to one woman who wanted to know if she was doing enough and making the proper progress in developing a career for herself in the arts. As she described it, her answer came back thus:

> I was going along a path when this woman came along, and was very practical and no-nonsense about telling me what to do … I asked her if I was really doing enough and making the proper progress in the arts. … So she said, "Don't worry about it. You're doing all you can. The main problem is that you worry too much. So don't worry." She was very straightforward about the advice she gave.

But was this good advice? The woman thought it was, because, she said: "I don't know what else I can do at this point to further my career. I'm making all the progress I can. This tells me I have to keep a balance between work and doing something that I like. That will help me stop worrying, like the expert said."

Interpreting Symbols

Should your answer come to you in the form of symbols or pictures, then you have to interpret them. In doing so, there is no particular thing that individual symbols or pictures mean. What's significant is what those particular images mean to you. It is possible that some images will reflect common cultural meanings for a particular image, since you are influenced by general cultural trends as well as by your own experience. You might see red roses as love, for instance, or champagne as victory.

The following example illustrates the process of reviewing the images you saw to interpret what they mean or how they answer your question. In this case, a woman at a workshop asked what to do about her fear of being more assertive in her job and her relationships. As she reported:

> I had a visualization after I asked about my problem. I found myself on a meadow or wooded area, and I met a very wise old guide, an Indian or the spirit of an Indian. She lifted her hand in an upward movement, and then she pointed ahead, and I saw water in front of her. Then, she moved forward towards the water, and it rippled, and I

felt like it was releasing the fears. Then, her hand went up in an upward movement, and I felt a sensation of power.

Later, this woman discussed her visualization and what she thought it meant. After some reflection and discussion, it appeared that the water was an image of cleansing and purification to her, as is commonly the case for water. The woman felt this meant she might imagine herself cleansing herself of her fears, and then she would feel more centered and wouldn't be blocked from acting because of her fears. This realization gave her a feeling of empowerment to deal with a troubling situation in her life.

In addition, since she had found an image that could help her release her fears now, it was an image she could use in the future with other fears. As I explained to her at the workshop: "Since that image of water is an image of cleansing and a release of fears for you, you can return to that lake whenever you feel burdened by fear. Just dump whatever fear is bothering you into the lake and watch it float away or sink. Then, you can walk away from the lake feeling released of your fear and cleansed."

Getting Your Answer in Feelings

Sometimes you may get an answer in the form of a non-verbal sensation or feeling. This can still give you a yes or a no. An example of this is the experience of one man who was wondering if he was going in the right direction in his life now. He found himself walking on a ridge. Then, though the guide he passed said nothing, he had a feeling that his guide was letting him know he was doing just fine. As he explained:

I was on a deserted ridge, and initially, I didn't see anyone else around. But after awhile, I saw this guru coming by and I told him my question had to do with directions and time. "I'm not sure what to do," I told him. "I feel like I've been moving ahead in my life, but I'm not sure if I'm moving in the right direction."

And then, somehow, I got an answer. There was no dialogue. But I got an answer that made me suddenly feel like I have been wanting to get away from things, and I guess my job is one more of those things I want to get rid of. But I also had a sudden feeling of security thinking about where I am now. I suddenly felt that I don't want to go on to another job. I'd rather feel that security of staying put for a while. And I felt like what I really need to do is slow down for now, just relax, and the ideas will come. When I'm ready I'll know where to go next. But for now, the message or more precisely the feeling was that I should stay there and just enjoy it more. I shouldn't take things so seriously. I should allow more vitality into my life. Now I do feel freer with what I'm doing, and once I'm finished with the job, I can move on.

Getting Your Answer From Multiple Guides

In some cases, you may find that more than one teacher or guide appears with your message. If so, this can be an even further reassurance that your message is a good one for you now; it's as if you have gotten confirming opinions from a number of doctors.

For instance, one man, who wasn't sure of what to do about improving his personal relationships, found a whole group of teachers surrounding him with suggestions. Moreover, they were all noted therapists, and since he worked as a psychologist himself, the appearance of many teachers from his own field was doubly reassuring. "They told me I needed to declare myself more, that I need to share more information about myself. They said I should express myself more and not worry so much."

Getting a Confirmation of
Previous Advice or Current Plans

Another way in which this technique is useful is to confirm ideas you already have, or suggestions you've received from others, about doing something. Then, your message can act as a go-ahead or give you reassurance about something you are thinking of doing but aren't sure. It's like getting the stamp of approval, because your guides or inner self are telling you clearly that what you want to do or have been considering is okay.

Of course, if you get a different message, this can suggest you need to look at things differently. You might look at the advice you have gotten from different sources more closely to sift and weigh alternatives. You might try some more visualizations to expand your own previous ideas or come up with new ones. Whatever you do, trust your inner expert to point you towards what you really feel is—or is not—the appropriate thing to do in the circumstances.

Getting Your Information in Different Ways

When you get information from your inner expert, teacher, or guide, essentially what you are doing is objectifying your own self. Sometimes it makes it easier to get that information from a "separate" inner self, so you can have a conversation or simply be receptive to this inner wisdom.

You may also get this information in different ways, since different people have different ways of perceiving information. Some people are very visual, and may see an image or picture of their expert. Other people may get this information verbally; they may not see anybody there, but they may hear what their expert is saying in the form of a voice. And other people may experience a sense of knowing or telepathic communication. So when you work with this technique, you may find that you get your information in differnt ways and that one way feels more natural or comfortable for you.

It doesn't matter which way you get your information— through pictures, through sounds, or through your senses. All are equally valid, so when you work with this technique in the future, use whatever feels right for you. This chapter has given you options in the ways you might work with your expert, whom to contact as your expert, and how you can receive information. It's up to you to select the approach that works best for you.

12

Turning Your Conflicts Into Creative Opportunities

As much as peace and harmony are ideals in relationships with others and for oneself, some conflicts are almost inevitable. When we relate to others, we encounter people with different goals, values, interests, and priorities. Even alone, we can be torn by different choices or uncertain about which of our different goals, values, interests, and priorities are most applicable in a particular situation.

A key goal of using the conflict resolution techniques described in this book is, of course, to resolve the conflict and restore harmony. Yet at the same time, you can use conflict as a source of learning and personal growth in a number of ways.

First, you can draw on the conflict to gain insights about yourself. You might use a conflict as an indicator that it is time to make major changes in yourself, in a relationship with others, or in an organizational setting. You might also learn from the conflict how better to deal with your feelings and to react in future conflict situations. And you might use a conflict to notice patterns of attitudes, interactions, or individual responses that contribute to more conflicts, so you can work on changing these.

See What You Can Learn

Conflicts can be turned into excellent learning experiences if you take some time later to look at what led up to the conflict and what happened during it. You can learn more about yourself, the others involved in the conflict, or the environmental setting contributing to the conflict. This knowledge might help you decide what to do in a particular conflict, and avoid a future recurrence. It might also help you notice recurring patterns, either with the same people or the same issues. You can examine what it is about a pattern that contributes to conflict, and perhaps alter the pattern, and thereby reduce or eliminate the potential for conflict. And you might look into the causes of the recent conflict to discover if you need to make larger changes in your life, your actions, or the friends and associates you choose.

In some cases, the recurring patterns of conflict you identify may be common ones. One woman realized that she was in a series of co-dependent relationships with men who had drinking problems. Barbara had low feelings of self-esteem about herself, and she found it made her feel better when she became involved with a man who needed her because of his own weakness. As the relationship continued, however, she would find herself angry at the man for being weak and not achieving the high goals she set for him. As a result, she would start nagging the man to pull himself together and work harder. He would fight back in return. Sometimes the result would be huge yelling arguments, even physical battles, leading Barbara to find herself battered and bruised. Yet afterwards they would make up, and once again Barbara would feel good because she felt her boyfriend needed and loved her again. The couple would settle into a new holding pattern until the next blowup, and so the pattern continued until there was so much hostility and confusion in the relationship that it just split apart. But afterwards, Barbara would find herself drawn again to the same type of man, setting herself up for a similar pattern of crisis.

What Barbara needed to do was look at these series of conflicts and identify the pattern, so she could work on breaking the cycle. One way Barbara found to do this is what many women in such co-dependent relationships resolve: to avoid such men in the future. If she sees a man has a certain type of character, she recognizes this quality and pulls away before she gets too involved. It was tough in the beginning for Barbara to do so, because this kind of interaction process had become a pattern which was filling her needs. But because she recognized the destructive pattern and fought against it, she was eventually able to pull away by finding other interests and building up her own self-esteem. The relationship she ultimately allowed to develop was much healthier and more fulfilling than those in her past, and much less conflict ridden.

In other cases, conflict patterns may be more personalized, but they, too, can be changed with some awareness and work. For instance, Philip reported difficulties that continued to surface in relationships with personal friends. He met many of these men at work or in social groups, and in the beginning they were drawn together because they shared many personal interests. Then, after they got to know each other a bit, they would open up and share some of their more personal concerns, such as their fears about jobs, their hopes for meeting women, their attitudes towards their parents, their future goals, just about anything. But after a year or two, Philip noticed, with one friend in particular, that a certain coolness seemed to develop, and he felt concerned that he and his formerly good friend were drifting away from each other.

What could he do about this? he asked at a workshop on managing conflict. The very process was happening in a current relationship, and he didn't know what to do. Philip said he valued the relationship a great deal, but he noticed that his friend was becoming reticent, withholding information and himself in their get-togethers. He was desperate to know what was wrong. Yet, he was afraid even to broach the topic at their weekly lunch together. "He might get upset and not want to answer," Philip said. Then, too, Philip was bothered by the fact that the man no longer seemed to be as interested in what he had to say, and seemed more exclusively focused on his own concerns (though Philip was hesitant to call the man's attention to this, too). Philip kept hanging onto the relationship by having the usual luncheons. Yet, at the same time he felt discouraged: the relationship seemed to be falling apart, and he blamed himself for having done something to cause this.

However, when Philip looked more closely at the situation in a workshop, he came to a number of realizations about this and other past relationships. He felt these realizations could help him have better relationships in the future, if not salvage his friendship with Philip. For example, he came to realize that the growing coolness which characterized the end of all these relationships was probably not because of anything he had done, so there was no need to blame himself. Rather, this was just the normal kind of drifting away that can occur in a relationship when people get involved in different activities and grow in different directions. Thus, it might be appropriate simply to relax, let the relationship go, if it seems natural to do so, and find another one to fill this need for male companionship. Then, too, Philip learned to recognize how he had consistently reacted to this process of drawing away by avoidance, even though he valued the relationship and wanted to keep it. He realized it might be worth it to let the friend he valued know what he really felt, and to explain that he was concerned about what was happening, so his friend might be willing to put more back into the friendship, too. Philip also came to realize that this drifting away might have to do with personal issues confronting his friend and nothing to do with him, so he shouldn't take what happened personally. Rather, he might offer to help his friend if he needed help.

These realizations, in turn, helped Philip to recognize that if he did value this current or any future relationship and he saw this recurring pattern of drifting away happening, he could bring it up with the friend and perhaps discuss what they might do to revitalize their friendship. If that didn't work, he could more comfortably accept that drift as something that was inevitable, though he had done what he could to preserve the relationship. That thought would help him feel comfortable going on to something new.

Even if there are no recurring patterns involved in a current conflict experience, you can use it as an opportunity to learn something about yourself and make decisions about future actions and directions. In fact, you might set aside some time to reflect on the problem. Think of all the ways you can learn and benefit from the current conflict situation, even though there may seem to be nothing good about the experience at the time. You may just be able to draw a silver lining out of the storm of conflict. This positive, solution-oriented approach might show you that the problem isn't as bad as you thought; and you might see all the change and growth that are possible.

Going Within Yourself After Conflict

One key to getting ideas on how to benefit from a conflict situation, or any other bad experience, is to look within yourself and seek some answers from your inner self. This will help you work through and process the experience, so you can learn from it and resolve it in your own mind. You'll feel more complete about whatever happened, and ready to move on. I have written extensively about the value of this process of looking within for answers and guidance in several previous books: *Mind Power: Picture Your Way to Success in Business* (Prentice-Hall, 1987); *Shamanism for Everyone* (Whitford, 1989); *Shamanism and Personal Mastery* (Paragon, 1990); and *The Creative Traveler* (Tudor, 1990).

If it helps to make the connection with your inner self, use visualization to get yourself into an altered state of consciousness. You can also try automatic writing to achieve this state; you just start by relaxing, with something nearby on which you can write. Then, in this relaxed, spacy state, you start writing, just letting the thoughts flow out. Write down whatever comes, without trying to analyze or judge.

This writing will not only tap into your unconscious, but will provide a record of what you think or observe, as well. However you reach this altered state, once there you want to think of the bad experience as a kind of picture in a frame. This way you can see it as apart from you, as if you are a pure observer, a moviegoer in a theater, or a reader perusing a magazine.

From this neutral relaxed state, you can look at what happened as if it happened to someone else. You can learn from it, examine what caused it, and imagine what you might do next as a result. The way to conduct this examination is to use your conscious, observing mind to ask the questions you want to know, such as: "How can I learn from what happened?" "What caused it to occur?" "What can I do differently in the future to avoid this problem?" Then, after you have asked your question, look at the picture or screen in front of you, and wait receptively for answers to come in any form. You may see a visual image or scene played out in front of you; you may see the words answering your question appear; you may hear a voice speaking the answer to you; and so forth. Different people have different ways of receiving information, and your answer may depend on whether your primary mode of reception is visual, auditory, or sensory. The important thing is to stay in this open, receptive state when you get your answers, so you can accept whatever comes. Later you can choose among these possible answers to determine what makes the most sense, much as in brainstorming for new ideas. But for now, just listen, see, or feel whatever comes.

When you are finished getting these ideas, it helps to imagine the conflict or bad experience out of your life for good. One way to do this is to use some physical gesture to sweep the bad experience out of your life. You might also visualize such an action. For example, if you have been looking at a picture or a screen in your mind, you might see yourself tearing up the picture, or you might see the screen shatter to bits or burn up. Such a visual image will help you believe the conflict is concluded, and no longer any part of your life.

Keeping Your Conflicts in Perspective

Sometimes the bad feelings generated by a conflict can throw you, so the conflict looms much larger in your mind than it really is and undermines your sense of direction or self-esteem. That can be a block to learning from conflict, in addition to making you miserable. For example, the woman described in Chapter 1 who was having a noise dispute with her neighbors kept a notebook of each hostile encounter she had with her neighbors. As the list grew in size, so did the problem in her mind. Soon she wasn't only thinking about the conflict when she was embroiled in it, but at other times during the day as well. She mulled over who did or said what, considered what she should do next in response, and alternately felt hostile, angry, or depressed every time she reviewed or anticipated a new blowup.

By contrast, if you can look at any conflict situation as only a small portion of your life and remind yourself not to let it grow larger, you can keep the problem manageable and in proportion. If you do find it difficult to contain the effect of a conflict situation in your life, you might attempt to deal with this in several ways:

- Try to bring the roots of the conflict out into the open, if you feel a discussion about what is going wrong might help to resolve the problem.
- Work on doing visualizations to help yourself detach from the conflict; use them to remind yourself that this conflict is confined to only one part of your life and shouldn't slide over into other areas.
- Remove yourself from the conflict situation if the other alternatives don't work; cut it down to size by getting rid of the day to day input that only feeds the bad feelings and thoughts about the conflict in your mind.

One typical situation where these strategies might be appropriate is at work, where there is a personality clash between people in the office. Imagine that a few people don't like each other; there is a feeling of tension as they work together. Overt expressions of conflict are infrequent and only last for a few minutes. But the feelings triggered by these encounters can grow and grow, so that they not only poison the working environment, but employees take those feelings home with them. And then those feelings at home can trigger a whole range of petty irritations that can erupt into still more conflicts, such as with spouses and children. Then *they* become upset and hostile. So the bad feelings and conflicts spread even more.

Hence, a single conflict can sometimes act like a seed that germinates, or like the germ of a disease that spreads, growing and passing on more and more bad feelings and thoughts. Thus, as soon as you see this happening, you need to implement a strategy of containment. Keep the conflict to one area and one issue; do what you can to resolve it; learn from it if you can; then put it away and move on.

Again, as you work with a conflict to bring it down to size, a visualization might be useful. For instance, see the tentacles of the conflict drawing back into the center of the original conflict, or see the new shoots of growth or the new invasions of disease being chopped off. As you imagine this cutting off or containment, you might review in your thoughts some of the key principles for keeping a conflict in proportion. Repeat them again and again in your mind, as a kind of affirmation, keeping the conflict down to size.

Some of the key principles to keep in mind to help you keep a conflict in proportion include the following:

- *Don't let a bad experience deflect you from your overall sense of purpose or direction.* The conflict may suggest you need to make a slight correction or that you need to learn to improve what you are doing in some way. But you can, and should, keep on going. See the experience as a challenge or a stepping stone to guide you in a new direction.

- *Find your own center or purpose and come from that; don't let other people's attitudes and expectations throw you off.* This reminder is especially relevant to conflict situations based on differences in values and goals. At times, you might find yourself thrown off kilter by a confrontation with someone else's views about what you should or shouldn't do. While it may be helpful to pay attention to different perspectives, you have to keep your own focus in mind too; don't let someone else's ideas displace your own.

- *Don't let a conflict or bad experience undermine your feelings of self-confidence and self-esteem.* It can sometimes be very easy to feel unnerved after a conflict, especially if you feel you have lost something or have given in as a result of the conflict. But try to disconnect yourself from the conflict, and try not to feel that your self-worth is invested in winning the conflict. The outcome of a conflict doesn't change who you are. It's something that happened; when it's over and resolved, it's time to move on. Remember that the deflation of self-confidence and self-esteem which sometimes occurs in a conflict is just a passing feeling triggered by the event. This will help you put the experience back in perspective. It's like the old gospel song by Johnny Cash: "This, too, shall pass." If you remind yourself of that when you're starting to let a conflict get to you, you'll feel better about yourself right away.

- *Remind yourself that a conflict experience is just a small percentage of your many experiences.* Still another way to cut a conflict down to size is to remind yourself that this is just a very small part of the sum total of the many things you are doing. Right after a conflict, you may tend to magnify it's importance and focus on the bad feelings that linger. You lose sight of the positives or the lessons that might come out of it, and that might still be possible if only you think about the conflict creatively. Accordingly, remind yourself that in time the conflict will sink back into its proper perspective among the many other things happening in your life. You just have to be willing to process it, learn what you can from it, and let it go.

Overcoming Negative Feelings

Sometimes it can be hard to find ways of learning from a conflict or putting the conflict experience in perspective because of the bad feelings spilling over from the conflict. Often the process of thinking about what you can gain from the conflict or how you can shrink it down in size will automatically release these feelings. However, when this doesn't happen, it may be necessary to take some steps just to let go of your feelings before you can put the conflict in perspective or learn from it. Time itself will diffuse many or all of these feelings; but the following suggestions are designed to speed up this process of letting go.

- *Forgive yourself.* A key reason you may feel bad after a conflict is because of feelings of self-blame. You feel that whatever happened was your own fault, or you feel that you might have acted differently during the situation to produce a more positive outcome. But the problem with these recriminations and regrets is that the event is over and you can't change it now. All you are doing is making yourself feel bad. Thus, if you catch yourself blaming yourself or thinking: "I wish I had done that differently; I know I could have; why didn't I?" short-circuit the process and stop the blaming. Instead of blaming yourself, you must learn to forgive yourself. This process of forgiveness is a central tenet in Roman Catholicism, among many other religions: after confession, for instance, a priest seeks a show of remorse, perhaps in the form of a penance, and then forgives. You must try to do the same. You might go through your own internal process in which you tell yourself what you feel you did wrong in initiating, participating in, or resolving the conflict. And then for each wrong, tell yourself: "I forgive."

- *Vent your feelings.* Besides feelings of blame which require forgiving, you may have other feelings left over from a conflict which also seem hard to send away. And you may find that thinking rationally about resolving the conflict isn't enough: the feelings remain. Perhaps, despite an agreement or a compromise, you feel so hostile that the conflict might erupt again. Or perhaps you feel discouraged and drained because of the battle, or just generally upset. Whatever your negative feelings, it can help simply to express and vent those feelings, so you can let them go. One way to do this might be to write about what happened in a journal. Another possibility is to find a quiet time to meditate and reflect on what happened, and notice the bad feelings that arise. Then, using your powers to visualize, see yourself taking those feelings into a sack. Imagine you are burying that sack in the ground or burning it up, so that those feelings will never again bother you. Through venting, you express and use up those feelings. Once free of them, you can go back and look at ways to work with or learn from the conflict in a more productive way.

- Others may be less critical than you think. Sometimes bad feelings flow out of a conflict because you think that people are blaming you for what happened, or because you think you showed a not-so-attractive side of yourself, and so you suffer a drop in self-esteem. One way to deal with this is to recognize that other people may be less critical of what you did than you are. It can help to recognize that you may have much higher standards than others, since you are judging yourself and your own ego is on the line. Then, too, it can sometimes help if you talk to the people you feel have bad feelings about you or the situation. You may find they don't have the negative feelings you feared after all. Or if you find that they do, you can make any necessary apologies or explanations, and thereby smooth those negative feelings out. Other people can be critical; but they should recognize and accept your humanness, which includes the ability to make mistakes.

- *Do something to take your mind off your feelings.* Finally, a good way to break out of the cycle of negative feelings is to do something active or physical. This will focus your mind on something else, and the shift in attention will help to dispel your negative feelings. A long walk, for example, has many restorative powers. Or if you can't sleep because you keep reviewing the conflict that just happened, you might get up and do something productive or something you like. Spend a few hours doing an involving work project; go to a movie; make or eat a food dish you enjoy; talk to a friend; plan a trip you might take. Whatever you do, the action should be involving. This will help stop your obsessing and make your negative feelings fade away.

Don't Let Others Hold You Back

One of the traps that can hold you back from dealing with a conflict situation creatively is the attitude of other people. Sometimes they may have a certain preconceived view of what you are or what you have done, and it may be very different from your view. This fact may have contributed to the conflict, and even after the conflict is over, that limiting view may continue to influence you. Accordingly, it is necessary to shake off that view. The first step is becoming aware that it is having a negative influence on you. Work on freeing yourself from the tyranny of other people's opinions, and especially those negative, self-defeating feelings that can stay with you. The following are some common views you might encounter and what you should do about them.

Avoid Negative People Who Won't Change

When a speaker gives a speech, he or she can easily be thrown off track by a person who is negative and disapproving. Some speakers get so concerned with trying to prove themselves to this person that they drain themselves of energy with the effort. At the same time, they end up losing the people who were positive and accepting in the first place.

It is the same if you are in a conflict situation. You may find yourself battling with someone who has a different point of view. Sometimes it can be helpful to look at how this person sees things; by feeling and expressing empathy for the other's point of view, you may be able to find a win-win resolution the other person can accept. But at the same time, there is a real danger in doing this: you don't want to go so far in looking at things from the other side that you forget about your own perspective. If so, you may find yourself accommodating the other person by giving up what you really value, because you have let the other person's view of you and your opinions put you down. If you see this happening, it may be better simply to pull away from the situation. Ask yourself if there is any point in struggling to change the opinions of negative people. It may be that their mind is already made up and they are set in their disapproval. If so, why struggle against it? If you can shift them around by a clear presentation of the objective facts of the situation, fine. But if not, let the conflict go and move on. The speaker would be wise to let a few hecklers go in order to please the rest of the audience. You too will get further if you focus on the people who are supportive and accepting of your point of view. So where possible, concentrate on relating to them.

Don't Waste Energy on Skeptics Who Won't Listen

Just as you can deflate yourself by trying to get the approval of someone who is determined to be negative and disapproving towards you, you can spin your wheels trying to convince someone who is skeptical and antagonistic to your point of view. Of course it can be worth it to have an honest and open discussion with such a person, because by sharing views you can both get ideas. But if after awhile you see that someone still holds rigidly to skeptical or critical views, and you just as strongly believe in what you are thinking or doing, it's probably best to stop trying to convince the person. If you do keep trying, your efforts are likely to lead to an open conflict; the person won't be convinced, and you will likely end up feeling drained of your energy, angry, hostile, or even worse. Such a conflict may only prove to be a quagmire that sucks you in deeper, undermining your sense of confidence and faith. That's not the kind of conflict from which you can learn and grow. The moral: be on your guard against die-hard skeptics and critics who don't seek to learn anything from your sharing of ideas and only want to prove they are right.

Don't Let Others Guilt-Trip You

Another way in which others can block you from dealing constructively with a conflict is by making you feel guilty. You are strongly aware of their condemnation or disapproval for something you did, or something they believe you did. This block is much like the hurdle of self-blame described earlier which requires self-forgiveness to overcome. The main difference here is that you are not blaming yourself; you're taking on the perspective of others who you think are blaming you.

Freeing yourself here requires two steps. First, you need to get rid of this other perspective and stop trying to see yourself through others' eyes. And secondly, you need to let go of the blame and the guilt. You might accomplish both by questioning what right others have to judge you or evaluate your worth. They don't see the whole you, made up of many motivations, interests, and needs, so they can't possibly understand you fully. There's even less reason for you to judge yourself by what you think others' eyes see, since you don't really know what or how they see. You are just making assumptions, and that's a risky game. Not only may others be wrong in judging you, but you may be wrong in judging their judgments of you. You can see how confounded all this can get. So distance yourself from any judgments by others, which are often as unknowable as they are unfounded.

If feelings of fault and guilt remain, even after you have released yourself from the view of others, you can go about freeing yourself through forgiveness. A gesture, expression, or ritual of forgiveness may help you do this. If you found visualization helpful in the past, you might try using a visual image: cleansing yourself of guilt in a purifying lake, seeing an object representing this guilt shatter or burn up, or imagining yourself being forgiven by an outside authority figure, teacher, or spiritual guide.

Talk to the Other Party

Still another potential block to moving on creatively and productively after a conflict is having bad feelings over the disruptions in human relationship caused by the conflict. These feelings might be worsened because you feel others have their own bad feelings leftover from what happened. It can be necessary to release these feelings before you can move on to look at the conflict constructively with an eye towards the future.

One of the keys to this release is being ready to talk to others who may have leftover bad feelings about something that occurred. You may feel that they are still angry, have lost respect for you, think you took advantage of them, or whatever. However, if you follow up and talk to these people a few days after the conflict occurred (giving things a little time to settle), you may find they don't have these lingering bad feelings towards you after all. Maybe you just imagined that they did, because that's the way you were feeling about yourself. On the other hand, if they do still have lingering feelings, you may be able to smooth the relationship over by showing your concern. This smoothing over can contribute to the process of feeling finished about the conflict and looking at it more objectively so you can learn from it and move on.

Summing Up

You can help turn your conflicts into creative opportunities by remembering the following points:

1. Look at the conflict to see what you can learn.
2. Go within yourself to get some ideas on how to benefit and learn from your bad experience.
3. Keep your conflicts in proportion by doing the following:
   a) Don't let a bad experience deflect you from your overall sense of purpose or direction.
   b) Find your own center or purpose and come from that; don't let other people's attitudes and expectations throw you off.
   c) Don't let a conflict or bad experience undermine your feelings of self-confidence and self-esteem.

    d) Remind yourself that a conflict experience is just a small percentage of your many experiences.
4. Overcome your negative feelings after a conflict through the following methods:
    a) Learn to forgive yourself.
    b) Take some time to vent your feelings.
    c) Recognize that other people may be less critical of you or what happened than you are.
5. Avoid the block of letting others hold you back.
    a) Be careful to avoid being sucked in by people who are negative or disapproving of what you are doing; focus on the people who are positive and accepting.
    b) Don't put too much energy into trying to convince the skeptics if they don't want to listen.
    c) Don't let others make you feel guilty for something you haven't done—or even for something you have.
    d) Be ready to talk to others whom you feel may have bad feelings lingering on after a conflict situation, so you can get rid of any misconceptions or smooth over any bad feelings.

———

If you are interested in contacting Gini Graham Scott about speaking, workshops, seminars, consulting, and training programs on resolving conflict, you can reach her in care of *Changemakers*, 308 Spruce Street, San Francisco, California 94118 (415) 567-2747; FAX (415) 931-8725.

Some Other New Harbinger Self-Help Titles

Scarred Soul, $13.95
The Angry Heart, $13.95
Don't Take It Personally, $12.95
Becoming a Wise Parent For Your Grown Child, $12.95
Clear Your Past, Change Your Future, $12.95
Preparing for Surgery, $17.95
Coming Out Everyday, $13.95
Ten Things Every Parent Needs to Know, $12.95
The Power of Two, $12.95
It's Not OK Anymore, $13.95
The Daily Relaxer, $12.95
The Body Image Workbook, $17.95
Living with ADD, $17.95
Taking the Anxiety Out of Taking Tests, $12.95
The Taking Charge of Menopause Workbook, $17.95
Living with Angina, $12.95
PMS: Women Tell Women How to Control Premenstrual Syndrome, $13.95
Five Weeks to Healing Stress: The Wellness Option, $17.95
Choosing to Live: How to Defeat Suicide Through Cognitive Therapy, $12.95
Why Children Misbehave and What to Do About It, $14.95
Illuminating the Heart, $13.95
When Anger Hurts Your Kids, $12.95
The Addiction Workbook, $17.95
The Mother's Survival Guide to Recovery, $12.95
The Chronic Pain Control Workbook, Second Edition, $17.95
Fibromyalgia & Chronic Myofascial Pain Syndrome, $19.95
Diagnosis and Treatment of Sociopaths, $44.95
Flying Without Fear, $12.95
Kid Cooperation: How to Stop Yelling, Nagging & Pleading and Get Kids to Cooperate, $12.95
The Stop Smoking Workbook: Your Guide to Healthy Quitting, $17.95
Conquering Carpal Tunnel Syndrome and Other Repetitive Strain Injuries, $17.95
The Tao of Conversation, $12.95
Wellness at Work: Building Resilience for Job Stress, $17.95
What Your Doctor Can't Tell You About Cosmetic Surgery, $13.95
An End to Panic: Breakthrough Techniques for Overcoming Panic Disorder, $17.95
Living Without Procrastination: How to Stop Postponing Your Life, $12.95
Goodbye Mother, Hello Woman: Reweaving the Daughter Mother Relationship, $14.95
Letting Go of Anger: The 10 Most Common Anger Styles and What to Do About Them, $12.95
Messages: The Communication Skills Workbook, Second Edition, $13.95
Coping With Chronic Fatigue Syndrome: Nine Things You Can Do, $12.95
The Anxiety & Phobia Workbook, Second Edition, $17.95
Thueson's Guide to Over-the-Counter Drugs, $13.95
Natural Women's Health: A Guide to Healthy Living for Women of Any Age, $13.95
I'd Rather Be Married: Finding Your Future Spouse, $13.95
The Relaxation & Stress Reduction Workbook, Fourth Edition, $17.95
Living Without Depression & Manic Depression: A Workbook for Maintaining Mood Stability, $17.95
Coping With Schizophrenia: A Guide For Families, $13.95
Visualization for Change, Second Edition, $13.95
Postpartum Survival Guide, $13.95
Angry All the Time: An Emergency Guide to Anger Control, $12.95
Couple Skills: Making Your Relationship Work, $13.95
Self-Esteem, Second Edition, $13.95
I Can't Get Over It, A Handbook for Trauma Survivors, Second Edition, $15.95
Dying of Embarrassment: Help for Social Anxiety and Social Phobia, $12.95
The Depression Workbook: Living With Depression and Manic Depression, $17.95
Men & Grief: A Guide for Men Surviving the Death of a Loved One, $13.95
When the Bough Breaks: A Helping Guide for Parents of Sexually Abused Children, $11.95
When Once Is Not Enough: Help for Obsessive Compulsives, $13.95
The Three Minute Meditator, Third Edition, $12.95
Beyond Grief: A Guide for Recovering from the Death of a Loved One, $13.95
The Divorce Book, $13.95
Hypnosis for Change: A Manual of Proven Techniques, Third Edition, $13.95
When Anger Hurts, $13.95

Call **toll free, 1-800-748-6273,** to order. Have your Visa or Mastercard number ready. Or send a check for the titles you want to New Harbinger Publications, Inc., 5674 Shattuck Ave., Oakland, CA 94609. Include $3.80 for the first book and 75¢ for each additional book, to cover shipping and handling. (California residents please include appropriate sales tax.) Allow four to six weeks for delivery.

Prices subject to change without notice.